Wind Power

by Peggy J. Parks

Energy and the Environment

ReferencePoint
Press®

San Diego, CA

© 2010 ReferencePoint Press, Inc.

For more information, contact:
ReferencePoint Press, Inc.
PO Box 27779
San Diego, CA 92198
www.ReferencePointPress.com

Picture credits:
Cover: iStockphoto.com
Maury Aaseng: 32–35, 47–50, 62–64, 76–79
iStockphoto.com: 13, 16

LIBRARY OF CONGRESS CATALOGING-IN-PUBLICATION DATA

Parks, Peggy J., 1951–
    Wind power / by Peggy J. Parks.
      p. cm. — (Compact research)
    Includes bibliographical references and index.
    ISBN-13: 978-1-60152-080-7 (hardbacks)
    ISBN-10: 1-60152-080-8 (hardbacks)
    1. Wind power—Juvenile literature. I. Title.
    TJ825.P343   2009
    333.9'2—dc22
                                                    2009001538

Contents

Foreword

66**Where is the knowledge we have lost in information?**99

—T.S. Eliot, "The Rock."

As modern civilization continues to evolve, its ability to create, store, distribute, and access information expands exponentially. The explosion of information from all media continues to increase at a phenomenal rate. By 2020 some experts predict the worldwide information base will double every 73 days. While access to diverse sources of information and perspectives is paramount to any democratic society, information alone cannot help people gain knowledge and understanding. Information must be organized and presented clearly and succinctly in order to be understood. The challenge in the digital age becomes not the creation of information, but how best to sort, organize, enhance, and present information.

ReferencePoint Press developed the *Compact Research* series with this challenge of the information age in mind. More than any other subject area today, researching current issues can yield vast, diverse, and unqualified information that can be intimidating and overwhelming for even the most advanced and motivated researcher. The *Compact Research* series offers a compact, relevant, intelligent, and conveniently organized collection of information covering a variety of current topics ranging from illegal immigration and deforestation to diseases such as anorexia and meningitis.

The series focuses on three types of information: objective single-author narratives, opinion-based primary source quotations, and facts and statistics. The clearly written objective narratives provide context and reliable background information. Primary source quotes are carefully selected and cited, exposing the reader to differing points of view. And facts and statistics sections aid the reader in evaluating perspectives. Presenting these key types of information creates a richer, more balanced learning experience.

For better understanding and convenience, the series enhances information by organizing it into narrower topics and adding design features that make it easy for a reader to identify desired content. For example, in *Compact Research: Illegal Immigration*, a chapter covering the economic impact of illegal immigration has an objective narrative explaining the various ways the economy is impacted, a balanced section of numerous primary source quotes on the topic, followed by facts and full-color illustrations to encourage evaluation of contrasting perspectives.

The ancient Roman philosopher Lucius Annaeus Seneca wrote, "It is quality rather than quantity that matters." More than just a collection of content, the *Compact Research* series is simply committed to creating, finding, organizing, and presenting the most relevant and appropriate amount of information on a current topic in a user-friendly style that invites, intrigues, and fosters understanding.

Wind Power at a Glance

Wind Power and the Obama Energy Agenda

In February 2009, President Barack Obama signed the American Recovery and Reinvestment Act, a $787 billion economic stimulus bill that includes $14 billion in tax incentives for wind energy facilities and other renewable energy sources. Additionally, the Obama administration's "New Energy for America" plan sets out long-term energy goals such as ensuring that 25 percent of America's electricity comes from renewable sources by 2025 and investing $150 billion over 10 years to stimulate private clean energy projects. The how, what, and when of such spending has prompted considerable debate.

How Wind Is Harnessed

Wind turbines are highly sophisticated machines with blades that capture the wind's kinetic energy, or the energy of motion.

Wind Farms

Huge groupings of tall turbines are clustered together to form installations known as wind farms, which may be located on land or in the ocean.

Benefits of Wind Power

Wind power is a form of renewable energy, meaning it will be available as long as the sun shines. Another benefit is that wind power allows countries to produce their own electricity, rather than being dependent on foreign sources for fuels that run power plants.

Use of Wind Power

Wind power is used to generate electricity, which means it can be substituted for all other electrical sources.

Viability as a Global Energy Source

Scientists and energy experts worldwide say that wind has the ability to supply the world with energy and that only a fraction of its true potential has been tapped.

Impact on Fossil Fuel Dependence

Fossil fuels are finite resources that will someday be depleted. Increased reliance on wind power could markedly slow their depletion.

Environmental Effects

Wind power is a clean source of energy that does not pollute the air, water, or land. However, turbines have been shown to pose a risk to bird populations and an even greater risk to bats.

Negative Perceptions

Some people object to wind power because they believe that turbines mar the natural landscape and are too noisy. Wind power can also potentially interfere with radar tracking of weather and aircraft.

Wind Power in the Future

Countries all over the world are increasingly turning to wind to generate energy, and wind power is poised to be one of the leading energy sources in the future.

Overview

66 The potential for wind energy is immense, and experts suggest wind power can supply 20% of U.S. and world electricity. 99

—Windustry, an organization that promotes progressive renewable energy solutions and empowers communities to develop wind power as an environmentally sustainable energy source.

66 A key challenge for wind energy is that electricity production depends on when and how consistently winds blow rather than when consumers most need power. 99

—Jeffrey Logan and Stan Mark Kaplan, energy specialists with Congressional Research Service.

For thousands of years humans have known about, and relied on, the tremendous power of the wind. In about the fourth century B.C., Egyptians built boats out of papyrus and traveled the Nile River in search of trade, rowing downstream with the current and using the wind to propel them back upstream. In ancient Persia, which is now Iran, people built windmills that resembled paddle wheels and used wind power to grind wheat and other grains. People throughout the Netherlands used windmills to grind wheat into flour, and then designed and built windmills that could pump water. Centuries later when Europeans settled in America, they used wind power to grind wheat and corn, pump water, and cut wood at sawmills. In 1888 Charles F. Brush, an inventor from Cleveland, Ohio, built the first large windmill that was capable of generating electricity—and that is when the real potential of wind power began to be realized. Today wind power is one of the fastest-growing sources of electricity in the world, and many scientists and energy experts believe that it holds tremendous potential for the future of energy.

How Wind Forms

Wind power would not exist without the sun. When the sun radiates energy toward the Earth, the water and land absorb its heat at different rates. Since land heats more rapidly than water, this causes portions of the atmosphere to warm unevenly. As the air above land grows hotter, it expands, and because hot air is lighter than the same volume of cooler air, the heated air quickly rises, leaving a vacuum in the space it had occupied. Heavier, cooler air rushes in to fill the vacuum, and this rushing motion is what is known as wind. At night the air over land cools faster than the air over water, which also influences wind by causing its direction to reverse.

Harnessing the Wind

Today's wind technology is highly sophisticated and utilizes machines known as wind turbines to capture the power of the wind. There are two types of wind turbines: horizontal-axis and vertical-axis, which differ based on their design and how they spin. Horizontal-axis turbines are the most common type, and the newest models tower over the landscape, with many standing more than 440 feet (134 m) high, which is almost the height of a 40-story building. The turbines are mounted on steel towers that are anchored in concrete for reinforcement, and at the top are three propeller-like blades that are typically made of fiberglass-reinforced polyester or wood-epoxy. These blades are often gigantic—the biggest wind turbines in the world have rotor blades that are longer than a football field. As wind flows over the blades, it causes a "lift," much like the wings of an airplane, and as the blades turn they collect

> " Today wind power is one of the fastest-growing sources of electricity in the world, and many scientists and energy experts believe that it holds tremendous potential for the future of energy. "

the wind's kinetic energy, or the energy of motion. The spinning of the blades in turn spins a driveshaft, which then transfers the kinetic energy to a generator, creating electricity.

Vertical-axis wind turbines, such as the Darrieus models that are named after French engineer Georges Darrieus, have curved rotor blades that go from top to bottom, which makes the machines resemble giant eggbeaters. Even though these turbines are not nearly as common as horizontal-axis turbines, some energy experts say they have great potential for the future, especially in urban areas where there is not enough space for large wind-turbine installations. According to energy researcher and writer Timothy B. Hurst, vertical-axis wind turbines can produce an estimated 50 percent more electricity per year than conventional turbines in the same amount of area and are able to generate electricity at lower wind speeds. They can also handle higher wind speeds than horizontal-axis turbines, which are designed to shut down automatically when winds are too strong. Hurst explains:

> Despite the ubiquity of the three-bladed turbine, the oft-overlooked vertical-axis turbines are making quite a splash in the world of wind energy, especially in small and micro-applications. So what's all the fuss about? Vertical-axis turbines apparently do not suffer from some of the same problems that plague small wind applications in urban settings, including aesthetic concerns, space requirements and sound levels.[1]

Wind Farms

The most economical and effective way to harness wind power is with clusters of large turbines known as wind power plants, or "wind farms," that are spread over wide expanses of land. Dozens of these huge turbines work together to provide energy to the power grid, which is a network of electrical lines that distribute electricity. The best places for wind farms are wherever the wind is strong and reliable and where there is plenty of wide-open space for turbines to be installed. One example is the Smoky Hills wind farm located in the Great Plains area of Kansas, which is the largest wind farm in the state. It covers more than 20,000 acres (8,100 ha) of land and features 155 wind turbines, each of which is 260 feet

(79 m) tall with blades that are longer than a 747 jet. Fully operational since the end of 2008, Smoky Hills generates enough electricity to power an estimated 85,000 homes each year. A much larger wind farm is located in the San Gorgonio Pass in Southern California. The facility has an astounding 4,000 wind turbines and generates enough electricity to power the entire Coachella Valley, where there are more than 117,000 households and 7,500 businesses.

Increasing numbers of wind farms are being built in the ocean, with turbines mounted on platforms that are driven deep into the seafloor. Many are installed miles away from the coastline so they can take advantage of strong oceanic winds without being visible from shore, and undersea cables carry the electricity to land, where it goes into the power grid. One such wind farm is Burbo Bank, which is located in the Irish Sea about 6 miles (10 km) off the western coast of England. The Burbo Bank offshore installation covers nearly 4 square miles (10 sq. km) and comprises 25 wind turbines, each

> " The most economical and effective way to harness wind power is with clusters of large turbines known as wind power plants, or 'wind farms,' that are spread over wide expanses of land. "

of which towers 459 feet (140 m) above sea level. Since the wind farm became operational in October 2007, it has provided electricity to an estimated 80,000 British homes.

According to a September 2005 report by the U.S. Department of Energy (DOE) and Massachusetts Technology Collaborative, there is tremendous potential for offshore wind farms in the United States. The report states that the capacity exists within 50 miles (80 km) of America's coastlines for more than 900,000 megawatts of wind generation. The authors of the report write: "Although there are significant opportunities for continuing wind energy development on land in some parts of the country, the future potential for offshore development may be even larger. The magnitude of the offshore potential rivals the current installed electrical capacity of the United States."[2]

The Benefits of Wind Power

One of the major advantages of wind is that it is a source of renewable energy, meaning it is continually replenished and will be available as long as the sun shines—and scientists say that will continue for an estimated 5 billion more years. Another benefit is that wind power allows countries to produce their own electricity, rather than being dependent on foreign sources, which is the case today with oil. According to the renewable energy group Windustry, this can result in substantial cost savings. Windustry's Web site explains: "Unlike other forms of electrical generation where fuel is shipped to a processing plant, for wind energy, the generating station, or wind turbine, is installed at the source of fuel. Wind is a native fuel source and does not need to be mined or transported, thus taking two expensive aspects out of long-term energy costs."[3]

The exploitation of wind power can also create thousands of long- and short-term jobs in the renewable energy sector for such positions as surveyors, structural engineers, assembly workers, technicians, and operators, among others. Windustry states that the potential for jobs is enormous when compared with employment created by other fuel sources: "Wind energy creates 30% more jobs than a coal plant and 66% more than a nuclear plant per unit of energy generated."[4]

How Wind Power Is Used

The primary use of wind power is the generation of electricity. In the same way that coal- or gas-fired power plants produce electricity for space heating and cooling, lighting, televisions, appliances, and innumerable other uses, wind power can do the same. The only difference is that the electricity is produced by wind turbines rather than at traditional power plants.

One wind power success story is Jiminy Peak Mountain Resort, which is a year-round resort facility nestled in the Berkshire Mountains of western Massachusetts. In August 2007 Jiminy Peak's 1.5 megawatt wind turbine known as "Zephyr" became operational. The resort was the first of its kind in the United States to install its own wind turbine. Today the Zephyr turbine —which is taller than the Statue of Liberty— generates a third of the resort's total electrical power.

There are other uses for wind power beyond generating electricity for homes and businesses. For instance, just as wind has powered boats for

This California wind farm features horizontal-axis wind turbines, which are sophisticated machines with blades that capture the wind's kinetic energy.

centuries, it can also help power land vehicles, and some of these are currently under development. One example is the Venturi Eclectic, a small vehicle that is self-sustained through solar panels on its roof and a small plug-in wind turbine that gives it an extra power boost when it is driven in windy areas. *Popular Mechanics* writer Brittany Marquis says that the Eclectic "looks similar to a squashed robot," and describes riding in it as "breezy, fun and actually quite exhilarating. Like all electric cars, it's very quiet and superbly smooth on the road."[5]

Can Wind Power Supply the World's Energy Needs?

Even with its vast potential, wind power may not replace all other energy sources because the wind does not constantly blow. Many scientists and energy experts are convinced, though, that wind has the capacity to generate a large percentage of the world's electricity—far more than is now being realized. Windustry states: "Modern wind turbines are up to the task of producing serious amounts of electricity. A popular sized machine in the U.S. today is a state-of-the-art 2 [megawatt] turbine that stands as tall as a 30-story building."[6] The group's reference to "megawatt" refers to how electricity-generating capacity is measured, which is in watts. A kilowatt is 1,000 watts, a megawatt is a million watts, and a gigawatt is a billion watts. Energy output is expressed in watt-hours; for example, a watt hour is equal to the power of one watt operating for one hour, whereas a megawatt hour is equivalent to 1 million watts operating for 1 hour. Windustry adds that with a good wind resource, one 2-megawatt turbine can produce 6 million kilowatt-hours of electricity each year, which is enough energy to power 600 average American households.

> "One of the major advantages of wind is that it is a source of renewable energy, meaning it is continually replenished and will be available as long as the sun shines.

Wind power use in the United States is growing rapidly. In 2007 the U.S. wind power industry grew by 45 percent, with more than half of that growth occurring in Texas. According to the Energy Conservation Office, Texas is the country's leading wind power state, "accounting for close to one-third of the nation's total installed wind capacity, which is the equivalent of the electricity needed to power more than 1 million Texas homes. A single megawatt of wind energy can produce as much energy [as is] used by about 230 typical Texas homes in a year."[7] Other states that are considered wind power leaders are California, Iowa, Minnesota, and Oklahoma, although a total of 34 states have commercial-scale wind turbines in operation.

Several European countries are much more reliant on wind power than the United States. For example, even though America has more installed wind turbines than Denmark, wind power accounts for less than 1 percent of U.S. total energy compared with Denmark's 20 percent. Another world leader is Germany, which generates about 7 percent of its total electricity from wind, while in some northern German states wind accounts for as much as 30 percent of electricity generation.

Can Wind Power Reduce Dependence on Fossil Fuels?

One of the major benefits of wind power that is often touted by scientists and energy experts is its nonreliance on coal, oil, and natural gas, which are known as fossil fuels. Currently an estimated 80 to 90 percent of energy production worldwide relies on these fuels, and although they are still plentiful in many parts of the world, they are finite resources that will someday be depleted. Since wind power is not available 100 percent of the time, it is not likely to replace these fuels on its own. But because of its vast potential for electricity generation, many scientists say that wind power could definitely contribute toward reducing dependence on fossil fuels, especially when combined with solar power and other renewable energy sources.

How Does Wind Power Affect the Environment?

There are numerous environmental benefits of using wind power as an energy source. It is a clean form of energy that does not require the burning of fossil fuels, which pollutes the land, air, and water through emissions of mercury, nitrous and sulfur dioxides, and other toxic substances. Fossil fuel burning also sends billions of tons of carbon dioxide (CO_2) and other greenhouse (heat-trapping) gases into the atmosphere each year, which a growing number of scientists believe is a major contributor toward global warming. A June 2008 report by energy specialists Jeffrey Logan and Stan Mark Kaplan states that wind power contributed about 32 billion kilowatt-hours of electricity to the U.S. electrical grid in 2007. They describe the effect this had on the atmosphere: "If that electricity had been generated using the average mix of power plants in the United States, an additional 19.5 million tons of carbon dioxide would have been released that year."[8] The DOE adds that if 20 percent of America's electricity was

> " Many scientists and energy experts are convinced . . . that wind has the capacity to generate a large percentage of the world's electricity—far more than is now being realized. "

Coal is moved from a mine by rail. One of the major benefits of wind power that is often touted by scientists and energy experts is its nonreliance on coal, oil, and natural gas. Fossil fuels are finite resources that will some-day be depleted.

supplied by wind (as is the agency's goal), this would reduce CO_2 emissions by more than 900 million tons (825 million t) per year.

Although wind power has many positive effects on the environment, there are some negative aspects as well. One of the strongest objections is that the huge wind turbines are dangerous to birds, which is true to an extent, but bird mortality is much less common than people may think. The DOE reports that the number of birds killed by wind turbines is a tiny fraction of those that are killed by colliding with buildings, windows, and vehicles. Perceptions about the risk to birds are largely due to older wind turbines, which had shorter towers with blades that were too close to the ground. Technology has continued to result in improved wind turbines that are taller and sleeker, and planners now have a better understanding of how and where to place installations so they will have a minimal effect on the environment, including bird populations. There remains, however, another environmental problem with wind turbines: Even modern machines are deadly to bats—for every bird that is killed by turbines, an estimated 10 bats are killed. Scientists are exploring this issue in an effort to resolve it.

Negative Perceptions

Whether wind turbines are a beautiful sign of renewable energy progress or a blight on the landscape is largely a matter of personal opinion. Many who object to the massive turbines believe the machines are unsightly and interfere with the natural environment. Others complain that wind turbines are too noisy, although modern turbines are much quieter than older models. According to the American Wind Energy Association, the newest wind turbines are "no noisier than a kitchen refrigerator or a moderately quiet room. The sound turbines produce is similar to a light whooshing or swishing sound, and much more quiet than other types of modern-day equipment."[9]

Beyond aesthetics, a more serious problem with wind turbines is that they have been shown, on occasion, to interfere with radar tracking of airplanes and weather, as Logan and Kaplan explain: "Wind turbines can interfere with civilian and military radar at some locations. The potential interference occurs when wind turbines reflect radar waves and cause ghosting (false readings) or shadowing (dead zones) on receiving monitors. Radar interference thus raises national security and safety concerns."[10] According to a January 2008 report commissioned by the U.S. Department of Homeland Security, a dead zone could result in radar being unable to detect intruding aircraft, as well as air traffic control software temporarily losing track of aircraft flying over wind farms. Scientists and engineers are aggressively studying this problem and are making a concerted effort to overcome it, either by modifying turbine designs, making changes in the aging U.S. radar infrastructure, or perhaps both.

> **Whether wind turbines are a beautiful sign of renewable energy progress or a blight on the landscape is largely a matter of personal opinion.**

A lesser-known issue with wind turbines is the adverse physical effects they have on some people, an affliction known as wind turbine syndrome. During a March 2006 testimony before the New York State Legislature Energy Committee, physician and scientist Nina Pierpont spoke about this medical condition and the risk posed by wind turbines. According to Pierpont, numerous people have reported symptoms that started when nearby turbines began operating and continued until the turbines were off or the complainants were away from the immediate area. Among their reported symptoms were problems with sleeping (the most common), migraines and other severe headaches, dizziness, nausea, exhaustion, anxiety and depression, problems with concentration, and tinnitus (ringing in the ears). Pierpont stated in her speech: "Not everyone near turbines has these symptoms. This does not mean people are making them up; it means there are differences among people in susceptibility. These differences are known as risk factors." Pierpont added that she supports the pursuit of renewable energy, including wind power, "which probably has its place, though that place is not near people's homes or near schools, hospitals, or other locations where people have to sleep or learn."[11]

What Is the Future of Wind Power?

Scientists and energy experts worldwide agree that the future of wind power is immensely promising. Although wind will not likely become the world's only energy source, it is widely believed that it has far more potential than is currently being utilized. Wind power will likely become part of the global energy "portfolio," along with solar power, geothermal energy (heat from the Earth's core), and other renewable energy sources— all of which would vastly decrease the world's dependence on fossil fuels. As technology continues to become more sophisticated, the challenges currently associated with wind power will undoubtedly be overcome, making this clean, renewable energy source even more valuable than it is today. As Windustry states:

> Technological advancements and supportive policy mea-
> sures have the ability to drastically increase the future of
> wind energy development in our nation and our world.
> Wind power has the unique ability to provide even
> greater sources of distributed energy production, which
> means less risk and a stronger energy portfolio. . . . Stay
> tuned to advancements at industry and policy levels as
> wind energy continues to grow.[12]

Can Wind Power Supply the World's Energy Needs?

❝Wind energy is the most attractive solution to the world's energy challenges. It is clean and fuel-free. Moreover, wind is indigenous and enough wind blows across the globe to cope with the ever increasing electricity demand.❞

—Global Wind Energy Council, an organization dedicated to the worldwide expansion of wind power, and Greenpeace, an international environmental organization.

❝Wind power cannot, by itself, totally satisfy the electrical needs of a city, state, or nation. It is at best a supplemental source, used in conjunction with fossil fuels, nuclear fission, and hydropower.❞

—Stan Gibilisco, electronics engineer, mathematician, and author.

The mid-1800s was a time of rapid settlement and growth in the United States. People throughout the country, especially those living in rural areas, became interested in harnessing wind for pumping water from the ground, and inventors aggressively sought patents either to develop new windmills or to improve on existing models. An American businessman named John Burnham envisioned a machine that was based on European designs but would overcome their shortcomings, such as automatically turning to face changing wind directions without human intervention. In addition, it would have the ability to control its own wheel speed so it would not be destroyed when winds were too strong, as was the problem with most windmills. Believing that he lacked the expertise necessary to design such a machine, Burnham approached an associate, Daniel Halladay, who was a mechanic from New England. Halladay was excited about the project and developed a prototype windmill in 1854. His design was precisely what Burnham had in mind, and it was unlike any windmills that had been developed before. Halladay was hailed for his creation, as one article in an agricultural magazine stated: "Daniel Halladay, a mechanic in an obscure country village . . . has done what the world of mechanics have sought in vain for centuries. He has invented and put in successful operation a windmill with *self-fueling sails.*"[13] In a relatively short period of time, the Halladay Standard windmill became a fixture on thousands of farms and ranches throughout America, especially in the Great Plains of the Midwest.

> " During the 1930s and 1940s, broad-scale distributed electricity became available, and the market for wind-powered electricity began to die out. "

Over the following decades, other inventors improved on Halladay's design, and the windmill industry in the United States thrived. The industry got an added boost when Charles F. Brush developed his electricity-generating windmill, and as more inventors created even better designs, windmills were in high demand. By 1930 there were an estimated 600,000 windmills scattered throughout America's countryside that were being used to generate electricity and pump water. Then, during the 1930s and 1940s, broad-scale distributed electricity became available, and the market for wind-powered electricity began to die out. Although windmills were still a common sight on farms and ranches, they were no longer the primary generators of electrical power.

Wind Power Leaders

During the 1970s, when the embargo imposed by the Organization of Petroleum Exporting Countries (OPEC) caused a steep, worldwide spike in oil prices, this spurred a renewed interest in wind power and other forms of renewable energy. As a result, a number of countries launched programs to develop wind turbines that were far more powerful than their predecessors. Although for many years the United States trailed behind Denmark, Germany, and other industrialized nations in the exploitation of wind power, by December 2008 the United States had become the largest producer of wind power in the world. According to the American Wind Energy Association, the projected capacity for 2009 is more than 60 billion kilowatt-hours of electricity, which is enough to power nearly 6 million American homes.

In recent years, as people have become more aware of the vast potential of wind power, it has emerged as one of the world's fastest-growing sources of renewable energy. The United States is one of the world's windiest countries—so much so that energy experts often refer to it as the "Saudi Arabia of wind power"—and many scientists say that the wind's potential has barely even been tapped. Yet even though the United States currently leads the world in *total* use of wind power, as well as new wind installations, with just 1 percent of electricity generation from wind power in 2008, the country lags far behind Denmark's 20 percent of electricity from wind power, Spain's 12 percent, Portugal's 9 percent, Ireland's 8 percent, and Germany's 7 percent.

> "In recent years, as people have become more aware of the vast potential of wind power, it has emerged as one of the world's fastest-growing sources of renewable energy."

The DOE has a vision for the future in which wind power will play a much greater role in United States energy generation than is the case today. In a report released in July 2008, the DOE presented an aggressive plan for wind to provide 20 percent of America's electricity by the year 2030. Based on projections by the U.S. Energy Information Administration, the country's demand for electricity is expected to grow by 39 percent, reaching 5.8 billion megawatt-hours by 2030. The DOE states that in order for wind power to meet 20 percent of that demand, its capacity in the United States would have to reach more than 300 gigawatts—which is a huge increase over what is being produced today. Although the

DOE acknowledges that this goal is an ambitious one, the agency is convinced that the achievement is possible with the right balance of commitment to wind power and substantial financial investments, which will be recouped through future energy savings.

Massive Wind Farms

Just as Texas holds the record of producing the most wind power in the United States (more than 3 percent of its total energy), it is also home to the world's largest wind farm. The Horse Hollow Wind Energy Center, located in Nolan and Taylor counties in Texas, covers about 47,000 acres (19,000 ha) of land and consists of 421 towering wind turbines. The installation, which became fully operational in 2006, generates enough electricity each year to power 220,000 homes.

The largest wind farm in Europe, the Maranchon wind farm located in Guadalajara, Spain, is one reason that country has succeeded in achieving an average of 12 percent of its total energy consumption from wind power. As impressive as that is, though, at times the percentage has risen much higher. For instance, on a weekday during 2007, Spain hit a production record that was an all-time high, with 27 percent of total energy consumption from wind power. An even more impressive statistic was recorded during a weekend in March 2008, when winds were especially heavy in Spain and the country achieved nearly 41 percent of total electricity consumption from wind power—and in November of that year, the amount rose even higher, to 43 percent.

Another European country that has aggressive goals for wind power is Scotland, where an estimated 16 percent of electricity is generated from wind and other renewable energy sources. The Scottish government's target is to generate 31 percent of the country's electricity from renewables by 2011 and to reach 50 percent by 2020. In July 2008 the government announced its approval of the Clyde wind farm, in South

> " The Scottish government's target is to generate 31 percent of the country's electricity from renewables by 2011 and to reach 50 percent by 2020. "

Lanarkshire, which will be composed of 152 wind turbines, be capable of providing electricity to as many as 320,000 homes, and surpass Spain's Maranchon installation as Europe's largest wind farm.

An Emerging Wind Power Leader

China is a developing country that is known worldwide for its heavy reliance on coal for nearly three-fourths of its electricity generation, much of which is used to power industrial operations such as cement manufacturing. Yet China is increasingly turning to wind power, with a spike in electricity generation from wind of more than 100 percent per year since 2005. Steve Sawyer, of the Global Wind Energy Council, says that the wind power market in China "is unrecognizable from two years ago [2006]. It is huge, huge, huge. But it is not realized yet in the outside world."[14] During the 2008 Olympics, which were held in Beijing in August of that year, 33 wind turbines located at the Gaunting wind farm provided 20 percent of the electricity used at the Olympic venues. Currently the wind farm provides electricity to 100,000 families, and this is scheduled to double when the second phase is constructed in 2010. Other large Chinese wind farms that are still in the development phase are planned for Inner Mongolia and the provinces of Gansu, Shandong, Heilongjiang, and Hainan. Energy experts from Inner Mongolia estimate that by 2010 the country's installed base of wind farms will generate 27,000 megawatts of electricity and that China will become the third-largest global producer of wind power by 2015.

> "One huge Danish offshore facility that is already operational is the Horns Reef wind farm, which is located in the North Sea about 12 miles (20 km) from the coastline."

In a paper published in June 2008, Junfeng Li, who is secretary general of China's Renewable Energy Industries Association, describes the country's commitment to wind power, saying that the recent boom in development has far surpassed the government's original goal. He writes:

China is witnessing the start of a golden age of wind power development, and the magnitude of growth has caught even policymakers off guard. . . . Wind power is said to already be more cost effective than oil, natural gas, and nuclear power generation in China. As the stability and predictability of the sector attract greater investment, it is widely believed that wind power will be able to compete with coal generation by as early as 2015. That will be the turning point in China, which by then will be the world's largest energy consumer.[15]

Offshore Wind Farms

Denmark, which already produces 20 percent of its total energy from wind power, has a particularly aggressive plan for the future. The Danish government forecasts that there will be a significant increase in the use of renewable energy in the coming years, and its goal is to increase wind power to 50 percent, or possibly even 75 percent, of Denmark's electricity consumption by the year 2025. The government expects to accomplish this largely with offshore wind turbines because Denmark is a small country of just 16,602 square miles (43,000 sq. km), and there is not enough available space for large wind farms to be constructed on land. One huge Danish offshore facility that is already operational is the Horns Reef wind farm, which is located in the North Sea about 12 miles (20 km) from the coastline. The 80 wind turbines within the Horns Reef offshore installation generate enough electricity to power 150,000 homes.

In June 2008 the largest offshore wind farm in the Netherlands officially became operational. Located in the North Sea approximately 14 miles (23 km) from the west coast of the village of Egmond aan Zee, the Princess Amalia wind farm is composed of 60 wind turbines and provides electrical power to 125,000 Dutch households.

An Energy-Independent Community

Massive land-based and offshore wind farms are being built all over the world and are a definite sign that wind power will supply increasing amounts of energy in the coming years. But sometimes the wind's vast potential to satisfy energy needs becomes apparent by examining smaller-scale projects that have resulted in energy independence. A prime example of this is the town of Rock Port, Missouri, which has a population of 1,300. In 2008, Rock Port officials announced that their town had become the first in the United States to generate 100 percent of its electricity through wind power. In fact, the four massive turbines located on agricultural lands within the city limits produce 16 million kilowatt-hours of electricity each year, which is about 3 million more kilowatt-hours than the town's homes and residents need. The extra 23 percent of electricity being generated is sold to the Missouri Joint Municipal Electric Utility Commission (MJMEUC) for use in other communities throughout Missouri. At down times when there is not sufficient wind for the turbines to generate at capacity, the MJMEUC reciprocates by supplying the town with electricity. Rock Port mayor Helen Jo Stevens is in awe of the success of the wind installation, admitting that she still wonders, "How did this ever happen to a little old town like ours?"[16] The progress that has been achieved by Rock Port may seem small when compared with the mammoth wind power installations that receive the greatest amount of publicity. Rock Port's achievement is significant, however, because it could very well be duplicated in hundreds of thousands of cities and towns throughout the world, rendering them self-sufficient in terms of the energy they need to sustain their residents' livelihoods.

> " In 2008, Rock Port officials announced that their town had become the first in the United States to generate 100 percent of its electricity through wind power. "

Looking Ahead

From the Halladay windmills of the mid-1800s to the sleek, modern, powerful turbines of today, wind power has long been recognized as an important source of renewable energy. Although the popularity of wind power waned during the mid-twentieth century, that changed in subsequent years as people became fearful of energy shortages and were more aware of how much more wind had to offer than they previously realized.

Today countries all over the world are aware that the wind has amazing potential, and they are aggressively tapping into that potential by constructing wind farms on land and in the ocean. But how much can people count on wind for generating electricity? Can it be depended on to supply the world's massive, growing energy needs? No one can answer those questions for sure. But if the heightened worldwide exploitation of wind power is any indication, it appears that wind will certainly play a prominent role in powering the future.

Can Wind Power Supply the World's Energy Needs?

Primary Source Quotes

66 The generation of electricity by wind turbines is dependent on the strength of the wind at any given moment. It is therefore variable, but not unpredictable. 99

—European Wind Energy Association, "Debunking the Myths," *Wind Directions*, March/April 2007. www.ewea.org.

The European Wind Energy Association refers to itself as the "voice of the wind industry," for actively promoting the utilization of wind power in Europe and throughout the world.

66 The viability of wind power depends on where, when and how strong the wind blows—none of which is predictable. 99

—Steven Milloy, "Junk Science: The Wind Cries 'Bailout!'" Fox News, July 10, 2008. www.foxnews.com.

Milloy is the publisher of JunkScience.com and DemandDebate.com and is an adjunct scholar at the Competitive Enterprise Institute.

Bracketed quotes indicate conflicting positions.

* Editor's Note: While the definition of a primary source can be narrowly or broadly defined, for the purposes of Compact Research, a primary source consists of: 1) results of original research presented by an organization or researcher; 2) eyewitness accounts of events, personal experience, or work experience; 3) first-person editorials offering pundits' opinions; 4) government officials presenting political plans and/or policies; 5) representatives of organizations presenting testimony or policy.

❝Some call the vast American prairie the Saudi Arabia of wind, capable of producing enough electricity to meet the entire country's needs—assuming there's the will to harness it.❞

—Steve Hamm, "Wind: The Power. The Promise. The Business," *Business Week*, July 3, 2008. www.businessweek.com.

Hamm is senior writer in *Business Week*'s information technology section.

❝The combined space for windmills and batteries would be just over half the land area of Rhode Island. Sometimes really good ideas have insurmountable troubles when real-world numbers are applied.❞

—Ed Hiserodt, "Making Renewable Energy Practical," *New American*, December 8, 2008.

Hiserodt is president of Controls and Power, Inc., and is involved with the design and development of electrical control systems for industry and municipalities.

❝After a decade of trailing Germany and Spain, the United States reestablished itself as the world leader in new wind energy in 2005.❞

—U.S. Department of Energy, *20% Wind Energy by 2030*, July 2008. www1.eere.energy.gov.

The Department of Energy's mission is to advance the national, economic, and energy security of the United States.

❝The U.S. wind industry has been crashed at least three times, quite deliberately, by Congress messing with the tax credits from year to year and in a stop-and-go fashion.❞

—Amory Lovins, interviewed by Michael Mechanic, "Power Q & A: Amory Lovins," *Mother Jones*, May/June 2008. www.motherjones.com.

Lovins is chair and chief scientist at the Rocky Mountain Institute, an organization that is dedicated to the efficient and restorative use of resources.

"While we may never have a society totally powered by wind, we could certainly use the uplift it offers."

—Derrick Teal, "Creating a Rustle: Why Some People Just Don't Like Wind," *Environmental Design & Construction.*

Teal is managing editor of *Environmental Design & Construction* and *Sustainable Facility* magazines.

"Wind turbines used to be noisy. This problem has been addressed over the years and modern turbines are quiet and have been compared to a kitchen refrigerator from a distance of 750 to 1,000 feet."

—Richard W. Asplund, *Profiting from Clean Energy.* Hoboken, NJ: Wiley, 2008.

Asplund is a professional energy analyst and advisor who specializes in clean energy stocks.

"One doesn't 'farm' wind any more than one 'farms' water in a hydroelectric dam. . . . These are large, industrial installations. They make large-scale, industrial noise. 'Jet engines' is the most common description I hear in surveying people—a jet engine that doesn't go away and which you can't get used to."

—Nina Pierpont, "Wind Turbine Syndrome," testimony before the New York State Legislature Energy Committee, March 7, 2006. www.savewesternny.org.

Pierpont is a physician and environmental scientist.

Facts and Illustrations

Can Wind Power Supply the World's Energy Needs?

- As of 2008, Denmark generated more than **20 percent** of its electricity from wind, followed by Spain (12 percent), Portugal (9 percent), Ireland (8 percent), and Germany (7 percent).

- The United States currently uses wind power to generate only about **1 percent** of its electricity.

- China's generation of wind power rose by more than **100 percent** from 2005 to 2007.

- The largest wind farm in the world is the Horse Hollow Wind Energy Center, located in Nolan and Taylor counties in Texas.

- Cumulative installed wind power capacity in the United States rose from 8 megawatts in 1980 to more than **24,000 megawatts** in 2008.

- The United States installed more than **5,200 megawatts** of wind power in 2007, expanding its total wind-generating capacity by **45 percent** and leading the world in new wind power installations.

- Worldwide, by the end of 2007 there were nearly **94,000 megawatts** of electricity generated by wind power, up from 59,000 megawatts in 2005.

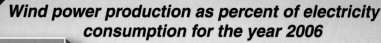

Top 10 Countries for Wind-Generated Electricity

Although the wind power industry in the United States has seen enormous growth in the past few years, some other countries use wind power for a much greater portion of their electricity.

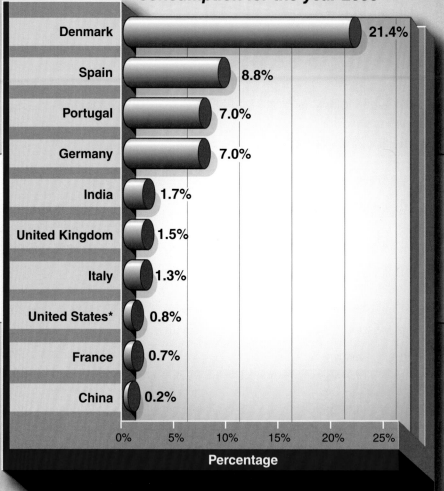

Wind power production as percent of electricity consumption for the year 2006

Country	Percentage
Denmark	21.4%
Spain	8.8%
Portugal	7.0%
Germany	7.0%
India	1.7%
United Kingdom	1.5%
Italy	1.3%
United States*	0.8%
France	0.7%
China	0.2%

Percentage

*Note: By the end of 2007, the United States had reached 1 percent of electricity generated by wind.

Source: Ryan Wiser and Mark Bolinger, "Annual Report on U.S. Wind Power Installation, Cost, and Performance Trends: 2006," U.S. Department of Energy, May 30, 2007. http://eetd.lbl.gov.

Growth of Wind Power in the United States

For many years the United States trailed other countries in its utilization of wind power, but since 2005, U.S. wind installations have grown at double-digit rates. This graph shows the rate of growth from 1985 to 2008.

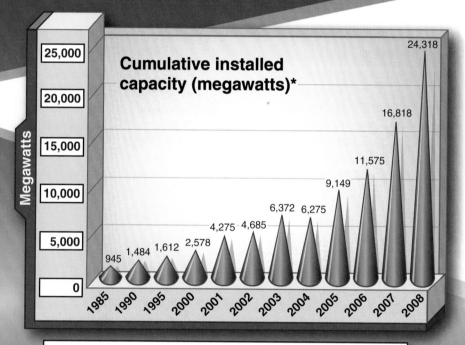

Cumulative installed capacity (megawatts)*

Megawatts

Year	Value
1985	945
1990	1,484
1995	1,612
2000	2,578
2001	4,275
2002	4,685
2003	6,372
2004	6,275
2005	9,149
2006	11,575
2007	16,818
2008	24,318

*Note: Electricity generating capacity is measured in watts and is an expression of instantaneous power output. A kilowatt is 1,000 watts, a megawatt is 1 million watts, and a gigawatt is 1 billion watts.

Source: Lester R. Brown, "New Energy Economy Emerging in the United States," Earth Policy Institute, October 15, 2008. www.earthpolicy.org.

- Large wind turbines require average wind speeds of **13 miles per hour**. If winds are not strong enough, the turbines do not generate power, whereas if winds are too strong, braking mechanisms cause the turbines to shut down.

Leading Wind Power States

More than 30 U.S. states have wind turbines installed, but some have been particularly aggressive at using wind power for electricity. This map shows the top 10 states for wind power generating capacity in megawatts* as of December 31, 2007.

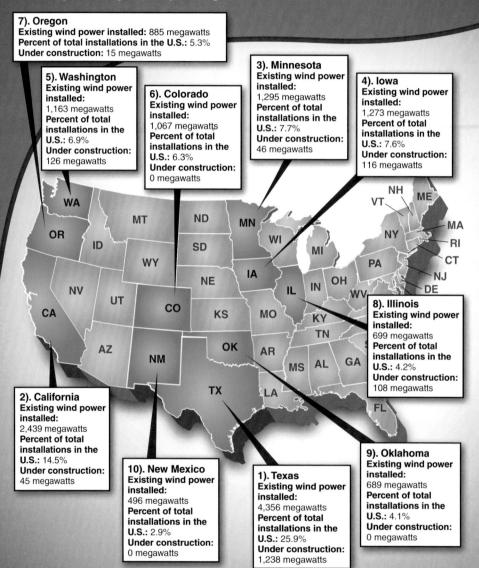

7). Oregon
Existing wind power installed: 885 megawatts
Percent of total installations in the U.S.: 5.3%
Under construction: 15 megawatts

5). Washington
Existing wind power installed: 1,163 megawatts
Percent of total installations in the U.S.: 6.9%
Under construction: 126 megawatts

6). Colorado
Existing wind power installed: 1,067 megawatts
Percent of total installations in the U.S.: 6.3%
Under construction: 0 megawatts

3). Minnesota
Existing wind power installed: 1,295 megawatts
Percent of total installations in the U.S.: 7.7%
Under construction: 46 megawatts

4). Iowa
Existing wind power installed: 1,273 megawatts
Percent of total installations in the U.S.: 7.6%
Under construction: 116 megawatts

8). Illinois
Existing wind power installed: 699 megawatts
Percent of total installations in the U.S.: 4.2%
Under construction: 108 megawatts

2). California
Existing wind power installed: 2,439 megawatts
Percent of total installations in the U.S.: 14.5%
Under construction: 45 megawatts

10). New Mexico
Existing wind power installed: 496 megawatts
Percent of total installations in the U.S.: 2.9%
Under construction: 0 megawatts

1). Texas
Existing wind power installed: 4,356 megawatts
Percent of total installations in the U.S.: 25.9%
Under construction: 1,238 megawatts

9). Oklahoma
Existing wind power installed: 689 megawatts
Percent of total installations in the U.S.: 4.1%
Under construction: 0 megawatts

Note: Electricity generating capacity is measured in watts and is an expression of instantaneous power output. A kilowatt is 1,000 watts, a megawatt is 1 million watts, and a gigawatt is 1 billion watts.

Source: Global Wind Energy Council, "Global Wind 2007 Report," May 2008. www.gwec.net.

Global Use of Wind Power Growing

Between 1996 and 2007, the world's use of wind power skyrocketed, increasing by more than *1,500 percent*. This graph shows the steady rise in installed global wind power.

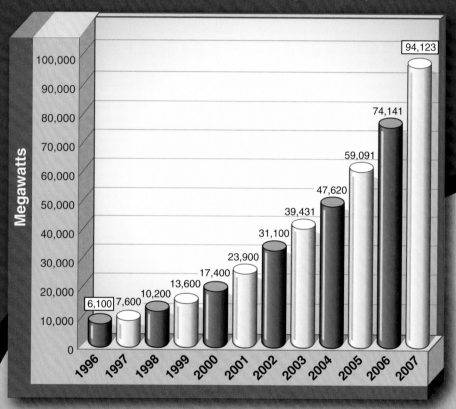

Note: Electricity generating capacity is measured in watts and is an expression of instantaneous power output. A kilowatt is 1,000 watts, a megawatt is 1 million watts, and a gigawatt is 1 billion watts.

Source: Global Wind Energy Council, "US, China, & Spain Lead World Wind Power Market in 2007," February 6, 2008. www.gwec.net.

- According to the American Wind Energy Association, **offshore wind turbines** generate more power than land-based turbines because wind speeds are generally higher and the wind is steadier offshore.

Can Wind Power Reduce Dependence on Fossil Fuels?

66In 2009 wind power is estimated to displace the burning of 30.4 million short tons of coal—enough to fill a coal train that would stretch 2,000 miles, from Washington, DC to the middle of Utah.99

—Environmental News Service, a daily international wire service that focuses on environmental issues.

66There won't be a single silver bullet to wean the world from fossil fuels, because they contribute some 80% of the present-day global energy supply, so the task ahead is enormous.99

—Richard Somerville, meteorologist with the Scripps Institution of Oceanography.

When people flip a light switch, turn up the heat, open the refrigerator, take a hot shower, or start a car engine, fossil fuels are probably the last thing on their minds. Yet none of the luxuries that are routinely enjoyed in today's society would be possible without fossil fuels: coal, petroleum (crude oil), and natural gas. Coal is crushed into a fine powder and then burned in power plants to form steam that generates electricity. Currently, more than 40 percent of the world's electricity is powered by coal. The primary use for natural gas is to heat and cool homes, schools, and businesses, and it is also used as a fuel for appliances such as water heaters, clothes dryers, and stoves. Crude oil is refined to make gasoline and diesel fuel for vehicles, as well as fuel for airplanes and jets, but is also used in numerous consumer products ranging from ink and crayons to vehicle tires and artificial heart valves. Together, coal, oil, and natural gas play a crucial role in the livelihoods of people all over the world and have enabled civilization to progress in ways that would never have been possible without them. Martin Hoffert, who is a physics professor at New York University, shares his thoughts: "This has been a great boon to our civilization, and we're really lucky. It's almost as if someone wanted us to develop civilization by giving us these fossil fuels. Without them, we never would have had the Industrial Revolution and we would undoubtedly still be living the way people did in the Middle Ages."[17]

> " None of the luxuries that are routinely enjoyed in today's society would be possible without fossil fuels: coal, petroleum (crude oil), and natural gas. "

Yet as much as fossil fuels are typically taken for granted, they will not last forever. Fossil fuels are a nonrenewable resource—and as energy demand throughout the world continues to spike year after year, they are rapidly being depleted. Because fossil fuels are finite, numerous scientists and energy experts tout the potential of wind power as an alternative source of energy. Even though wind may never completely eliminate the world's reliance on fossil fuels, it has the potential to reduce dependence on them and slow their depletion.

Remnants of an Ancient Past

Although fossil fuels each have different properties, their formation began in much the same way. About 300 million years ago, Earth's landmasses were just beginning to form, and the world did not look anything like it does today. The land was covered in swamps and bogs, with huge trees, mosses, ferns, and other plant life growing in and around the water and thriving in the warm, moist climate. As living organisms died, they began to decompose and over time were buried under deep layers of mud, rock, clay, and sand. Additional layers of sediment continued to pile on top of the organic materials, which squeezed them tightly, creating immense heat and pressure. Over millions of years, the decomposed organisms underwent chemical transformation and eventually became fossil fuels.

Certain factors influenced which type of fossil fuel formed. For example, most scientists believe that coal formed from the remains of trees, ferns, and other types of plants that grew in swamps and bogs or along shorelines. In some areas the decomposed vegetation sank to the bottom of swamps that were covered by seawater, and because the water was salty, it contained high amounts of the chemical element sulfur. When the seas dried up, the coal that formed contained high levels of sulfur. Coal also formed in areas where there were freshwater swamps, but it had a much lower sulfur content.

> " Among the scientific community it is widely believed that oil formed from algae and other microscopic organisms that lived in oceans and rivers. "

Oil and natural gas were created by the same basic forces, although there were some differences. Among the scientific community it is widely believed that oil formed from algae and other microscopic organisms that lived in oceans and rivers. "Long after the great prehistoric seas and rivers vanished," the DOE writes, "heat, pressure and bacteria combined to compress and 'cook' the organic material under layers of silt. In most areas . . . oil formed first, but in deeper, hot regions underground, the cooking process continued until natural gas was formed."[18]

As time passed some oil and natural gas percolated up through the Earth's crust until the fuels were trapped by hard rock formations known as cap rock, which prevented them from traveling farther upward and seeping through the surface. But in other cases, the fuels did make their way to the surface. For example, the ancient Egyptians discovered oil oozing from the ground and, believing it had medicinal properties, used it as a treatment for wounds. North American natives found oil floating on the top of streams and lakes, and after skimming it off with blankets, used it to waterproof their canoes. Natural gas also seeped from cracks in the ground during ancient times, and it frightened people because lightning strikes sometimes caused it to burst into flames.

How Fossil Fuels Are Found

Geologists use a number of sophisticated methods to locate oil, coal, and natural gas deposits buried in the Earth. To look for oil, for instance, they search for regions throughout the world where rock formations that are known to trap oil are located. Once such an area has been discovered, an oil company may drill an exploratory well to remove rock samples, which are then examined under a microscope to detect tiny oil droplets trapped inside the rock. Another method of locating oil is with devices known as geophones that send sound waves through the rock. Scientists can measure the speed at which the sound waves travel in order to determine whether oil might be contained in them. If it is determined that there is oil, oil companies drill wells deep into the rock so the fuel can be pumped out.

Because coal beds are typically enormous, scientists have already identified most of the world's largest coal resources, which are most plentiful in Europe, the Asia-Pacific region, and North America. Several different methods are used to remove coal, such as digging mines underground and removing the coal with huge machines known as longwall miners that use rotating drums to rip large chunks of coal from seams in the mine. Another method is known as surface mining, where coal beds are blasted apart with dynamite and mammoth, earth-moving shovels scoop up the coal and load it onto trucks.

Decreasing Supply of Fossil Fuels

Although few would argue that coal, oil, and natural gas are finite resources, scientists do not necessarily agree on how much of these fuels remain in the earth. Hoffert says that coal is the most abundant fossil fuel, with enough reserves left to last a few hundred more years. He adds that there is much less oil and natural gas, which he believes will be used up before the end of the twenty-first century. He explains: "It took hundreds of millions of years for fossil fuel reserves to form, and we're using them up a million times faster than nature made them! As the worldwide demand for energy continues to grow, these fuels are being removed from the ground at an increasingly rapid rate—and when they're gone, they're gone."[19]

A June 2008 report by British Petroleum (BP) provides an in-depth analysis of fossil fuels and states that at the end of 2007, worldwide oil reserves totaled just over 1.2 trillion barrels. That may sound like a massive amount, and indeed it is—until one considers that every year the world is consuming oil more rapidly than it is being produced. BP reports that during 2007, global consumption grew by a million barrels per day, while production fell by 130,000 barrels per day. The same was true for coal, for which consumption was 3.5 billion tons (3.2 billion t) compared with production of 3.4 billion tons (3.1 billion t). According to BP, worldwide consumption of coal rose during 2007 for the fifth consecutive year, with China accounting for more than 50 percent of the coal that was consumed. Natural gas was the only fossil fuel with production rates that slightly exceeded consumption during 2007.

> **A June 2008 report by British Petroleum (BP) provides an in-depth analysis of fossil fuels and states that at the end of 2007, worldwide oil reserves totaled just over 1.2 trillion barrels.**

One of the biggest problems inherent in the world's reliance on fossil fuels is that coal, oil, and natural gas are unevenly distributed, which means that many countries are highly dependent on foreign sources. For instance, of the 1.2 trillion barrels of oil reported as reserves by BP, more than 755 billion barrels were located in the Middle East, while fewer than 70 billion barrels were in North America. The United States is the world's biggest consumer of oil, with imports of more than 65 percent from other countries—yet during some months, the amount of oil that America imports is significantly higher. For instance, the U.S. Energy Information Administration reports that during October 2008, approximately 86 percent of America's oil came from Canada, Saudi Arabia, Mexico, Iraq, and 6 other countries. Conversely, the United States is richer in coal resources than any country in the world, and regularly exports coal to Canada, Mexico, and countries in South America, Europe, Asia, and Africa.

Challenges of Replacing Fossil Fuels

The rapid depletion of coal, oil, and natural gas is a major reason increasing numbers of scientists and energy experts are advocating greater reliance on wind power and other forms of renewable energy. Hoffert shares his thoughts: "My opinion is that we need to get to the point where we stop using fossil fuels. . . . I believe that if we really wanted to, we could run the world on wind and solar energy." He adds, however, that a total switch to renewables would present some tough challenges: "The main problem is the fact that we don't have an infrastructure that can absorb them. The electric distribution grid that we currently have was originally built a hundred years ago, and in order to assimilate wind and solar power into it, and have a system that can store and distribute energy to millions of people, the grid needs to be redesigned and rebuilt."[20]

An August 2008 article in the *New York Times* focused on the limitations of America's power grid and used the Maple Ridge Wind Farm in upstate New York to illustrate the magnitude of the problem. It cost $320 million to build the wind farm, which became operational in 2006. With nearly 200 wind turbines, Maple Ridge is New York's largest wind power facility. After construction was complete, the wind farm was expected to

> **The rapid depletion of coal, oil, and natural gas is a major reason increasing numbers of scientists and energy experts are advocating greater reliance on wind power and other forms of renewable energy.**

quadruple the state's wind energy capacity. At times, however, regional electric lines became overly congested and the facility was forced to shut down—and unfortunately, this is a common concern that plagues many wind farms. The DOE estimates that in order to achieve its 20 percent wind power goal by 2030, 12,000 miles (19,000 km) of new transmission lines would need to be constructed at a cost of about $20 billion. Some energy experts say that the cost could be considerably higher, but without that sort of radical overhaul to the electric grid, the full potential of wind power will likely never be realized.

Another challenge of switching to wind power is that the construction of huge wind farms costs hundreds of millions of dollars, and that is one of the wind industry's major roadblocks. In addition to high start-up costs, wind power production costs more per kilowatt-hour than fossil fuels. Coal, for instance, is currently a cheaper alternative for producing electricity. It costs Kansas-based Sunflower Electric Power about 1.5 cents per kilowatt-hour to produce electricity at coal-fired power plants and an estimated 4.5 cents per kilowatt-hour for the electricity it buys from wind farms. But this cost discrepancy is starting to change, partly because as coal supplies continue to be depleted, the cost of coal is rising. Also, as wind power becomes more prevalent, this causes the cost of wind-generated electricity to drop. According to Windustry, the cost of electricity produced from wind has fallen from 30 cents per kilowatt-hour in the 1980s to 3 to 5 cents today, and as technology continues to improve, the cost will decrease even more. Wind power will also reduce dependence on foreign oil sources and keep energy costs from rising and falling at erratic rates, as Windustry explains: "Wind energy is homegrown electricity, and can help control spikes in fossil fuel costs."[21]

> " Another challenge of switching to wind power is that the construction of huge wind farms costs hundreds of millions of dollars, and that is one of the wind industry's major roadblocks. "

Moving Forward

Fossil fuels are essential to the modern way of life that people throughout the world enjoy, and reducing dependence on them will be a daunting task that will undoubtedly take many years and incur an enormous expense. Will wind power be capable of filling this gap? Does wind power really have the potential to replace today's innumerable worldwide uses for fossil fuels? The fact is, no one can answer those questions with any certainty. But it is widely known that fuel consumption is continuing to outpace production year after year, and coal, oil, and natural gas are finite resources that are being depleted at unprecedented rates. Whether people agree about wind power or not, there is little disagreement that something must be done to wean the world from fossil fuels—because the future depends on it.

Primary Source Quotes*

Can Wind Power Reduce Dependence on Fossil Fuels?

66Supplies of all fossil fuels—oil, gas and coal—are becoming scarcer and more expensive to produce. . . . By contrast, the reserves of renewable energy that are technically accessible globally are large enough to provide about six times more power than the world currently consumes—forever.**99**

—Sven Teske, *Energy [R]evolution*, October 2008. www.greenpeace.org.

Teske is the international renewable energy director with Greenpeace.

66The industry is unable to show any evidence that wind power on the grid reduces the use of other fuels.**99**

—National Wind Watch, "Low Benefit—Huge Negative Impact," 2006. www.wind-watch.org.

National Wind Watch is a coalition of groups and individuals who seek to promote awareness of and document the negative effects of industrial-scale wind turbines on the environment, economy, and quality of life.

Bracketed quotes indicate conflicting positions.

* Editor's Note: While the definition of a primary source can be narrowly or broadly defined, for the purposes of Compact Research, a primary source consists of: 1) results of original research presented by an organization or researcher; 2) eyewitness accounts of events, personal experience, or work experience; 3) first-person editorials offering pundits' opinions; 4) government officials presenting political plans and/or policies; 5) representatives of organizations presenting testimony or policy.

"The growing global demand for energy in all of its forms is naturally putting pressure on the declining supplies of traditional fossil fuels, particularly crude oil and natural gas."

—Robert L. Evans, *Fueling Our Future*. New York: Cambridge University Press, 2007.

Evans is director of the Clean Energy Research Center at the University of British Columbia.

"In less time than has passed since the founding of Jamestown, today's coal reserves will be forever gone."

—John C. Mankins, "Energy from Orbit," *Ad Astra*, Spring 2008. www.nss.org.

Mankins is president of Artemis Innovation Management Solutions and a recognized leader in space systems and technology innovation.

"Creating a new energy economy isn't just a challenge to meet, it's an opportunity to seize—an opportunity that will create new businesses, new industries, and millions of new jobs."

—Barack Obama, "New Energy for America," speech given at Michigan State University, August 4, 2008. http://thepage.time.com.

Obama is the forty-fourth president of the United States.

"Obama's 'green jobs' plan would indeed create jobs, but it would do so by killing other jobs. Is that really the type of energy policy Americans want?"

—Kenneth P. Green, "Obama's 'Green Jobs' Plan Will Not Work," *On the Issues*, November 2008. www.aei.org.

Green is a resident scholar at the American Enterprise Institute for Public Policy Research.

❝Global climate change, in particular the prospect for global warming, has put the spotlight on our large appetite for fossil fuels.❞

—Robert L. Evans, *Fueling Our Future.* New York: Cambridge University Press, 2007.

Evans is director of the Clean Energy Research Center at the University of British Columbia.

❝Given rising prices for coal, natural gas, and nuclear fuel, power suppliers are drawn to the certainty that wind—while variable—is inexhaustible and has no fuel cost.❞

—Jeffrey Logan and Stan Mark Kaplan, "Wind Power in the United States: Technology, Economic, and Policy Issues," *CRS Report for Congress*, June 20, 2008. www.fas.org.

Logan and Kaplan are energy policy specialists with the Resources, Science, and Industry Division of the Federation of American Scientists.

Can Wind Power Reduce Dependence on Fossil Fuels?

- According to a January 2009 report from the World Wind Energy Association, at the end of 2008 wind power provided more than **1.5 percent** of worldwide electricity consumption.

- The World Coal Institute estimates that coal furnishes **93 percent** of electricity for both Poland and South Africa, **80 percent** for Australia, **78 percent** for China, **71 percent** for Israel, and **69 percent** for India.

- A June 2008 report by British Petroleum showed that worldwide oil reserves totaled just over **1.2 trillion** barrels; natural gas totaled **231 trillion cubic yards** (177 trillion cu. m), and coal totaled **934 billion tons** (847 billion t).

- The United States is the world's biggest consumer of oil, importing more than **65 percent** from Canada, Saudi Arabia, Mexico, Iraq, and other countries.

- Of the total world electricity generation in 2006, **coal** produced the largest amount (**41 percent**).

- Worldwide coal consumption rose during 2007 for the fifth consecutive year, with **China** accounting for more than **50 percent** of coal usage.

World Energy Breakdown

The use of wind power and other renewable energy sources continues to grow each year, but fossil fuels (coal, oil, and natural gas) produce exponentially more of the world's energy. These charts show what resources are used to produce electricity worldwide, as well as in the United States.

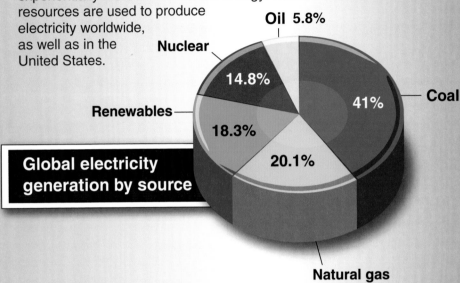

Oil 5.8%

Nuclear 14.8%

Renewables 18.3%

20.1%

41% — **Coal**

Global electricity generation by source

Natural gas

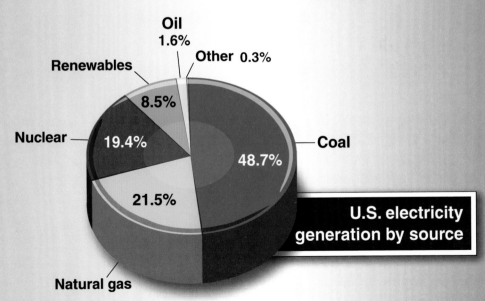

Oil 1.6%

Other 0.3%

Renewables 8.5%

Nuclear 19.4%

21.5%

48.7%

— **Coal**

U.S. electricity generation by source

Natural gas

Sources: World Coal Institute, "Coal Facts," 2008. www.worldcoal.org; U.S. Energy Administration, "How Is My Electricity Generated, Delivered, and Priced?" July 10, 2008. http://tonto.eia.doe.gov.

The World's Insatiable Appetite for Fossil Fuels

Fossil fuels (coal, oil, and natural gas) began to form hundreds of millions of years ago from the fossilized remains of living organisms. Although they are still plentiful throughout the world, they are finite resources, meaning that they will someday be depleted—and as global consumption of these fuels continues to increase year after year, they are rapidly being used up. These graphs show the global consumption rates from 1980 to 2006.

Worldwide coal consumption (in millions of tons)

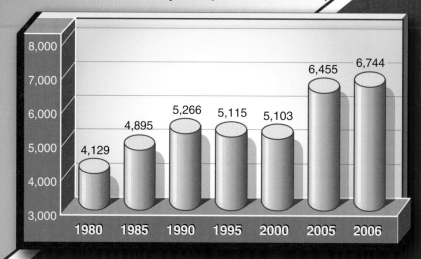

Worldwide oil consumption (in thousands of barrels per day)

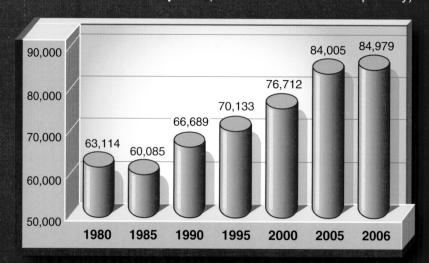

Worldwide natural gas consumption (in trillions of cubic feet)

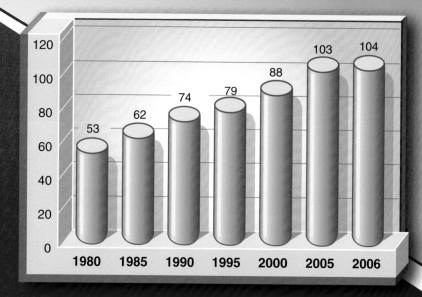

Source: U.S. Energy Information Administration, *International Energy Annual 2006*, December 31, 2008. www.eia.doe.gov.

- Many scientists estimate that **coal reserves** will last for several hundred more years, while oil and gas will be **depleted by the end of the twenty-first century**.

- A study released in 2008 by the European Renewable Energy Council showed that the world could **halt fossil fuel** use by 2090.

How a Wind Turbine Generates Electricity

This illustration shows how a wind turbine works. First, wind must blow on the blades to make them turn; 2. The blades turn a shaft inside the box at the top of the turbine; 3. The shaft goes into the gearbox which increases the rotation speed enough for; 4. the generator, which uses magnetic fields to convert the rotational energy to electrical energy. 5. The power output goes into a transformer, which converts the electricity coming out of the generator to the correct voltage for the distribution system. 6. The national grid transmits the power around the country.

Source: British Wind Energy Association, "How Does Wind Energy Work?" 2007. www.bwea.com.

- Jobs in the coal mining industry have remained steady in recent years, but are down by nearly **50 percent** since 1986.

- A report by the University of Massachusetts stated that investing in wind and other renewable energy sources would create **four times as many jobs** as similar investments in the oil industry.

How Does Wind Power Affect the Environment?

For those who are most enthusiastic about wind power, the fact that wind is a clean, nonpolluting energy source is among its greatest benefits—which is in stark contrast to fossil fuels. In order to release the energy that is stored within coal, oil, and natural gas, the fuels must be burned, which pollutes the air, water, and land. The Alliance for Clean Energy New York contrasts the positive environmental effects of wind power with the damage caused by fossil fuels:

> Because wind energy can displace other, more damaging energy sources, it helps to protect air and water quality, fight global warming, and reduce the need to mine and

drill for natural gas, coal, and other fuels. In fact, generating the same amount of electricity as 10,000 MW of wind power would require burning more than 12 million tons of coal . . . or 40 million barrels of oil each year.[22]

The Dirtiest Fuel

Since the primary use for wind power is generating electricity, many scientists and environmental groups hope that it will someday make the need for coal obsolete. That will be a monumental task, however, because people all over the world depend on coal for electrical power. Currently, coal-fired power plants generate nearly 50 percent of the electricity in the United States, and in some countries the reliance on coal is much greater. According to the World Coal Institute, coal furnishes 93 percent of electricity for Poland, 93 percent for South Africa, 80 percent for Australia, 78 percent for China, 71 percent for Israel, and 69 percent for India.

Of all the fossil fuels, coal is, by far, the most harmful for the environment because whenever it is burned, enormous amounts of sulfur dioxide and other toxic substances are released into the atmosphere. There are thousands of coal-fired power plants throughout the world, and according to the Worldwatch Institute, just one of these power plants can emit as much as 30,000 tons (27,200 t) of sulfur dioxide into the air each year.

> " Since the primary use for wind power is generating electricity, many scientists and environmental groups hope that it will someday make the need for coal obsolete. "

One of the most destructive results of this sort of pollution is acid rain, which forms when toxic gases mix with water, oxygen, and other chemicals in the atmosphere and change into corrosive acidic compounds. Acid rain (which includes other types of precipitation such as snow, sleet, and fog) can severely damage everything that comes in contact with it. It can eat away and eventually destroy sculptures, monuments, and cemetery headstones, as well as cause bridges to collapse. It strips trees of their leaves and needles and eventually kills them. This has occurred in the northeastern part of the United States, where entire forests have been destroyed by acid rain, such as in New York's Adirondack Mountains, where more than half of the red spruce trees have been killed. Acid rain also turns lakes and streams into acidic bodies of water, making them uninhabitable for fish and other wildlife. According to a study by the U.S. Geological Survey, two-thirds of the streams in the Adirondacks have been polluted by acid rain.

> " **Nowhere is environmental damage from coal-burning industries more apparent than in China, which has some of the most polluted cities in the world.** "

Nowhere is environmental damage from coal-burning industries more apparent than in China, which has some of the most polluted cities in the world. China relies on coal for nearly 80 percent of its energy, and industries powered by coal have wreaked havoc on the environment. A June 2006 *New York Times* article describes what has happened throughout China as a result of its heavy reliance on coal: "The coal-mining operations have damaged waterways and scarred the land. Because of intense underground mining, thousands of acres are prone to sinking, and hundreds of villages are blackened with coal waste. . . . Roads are covered in coal tar; houses are coated with soot . . . the air is thick with the smell of burning coal."[23] Studies have shown that each year, an estimated 400,000 Chinese people die prematurely as a result of illnesses that stem from sulfur dioxide, the result of coal combustion's pollution of the air. China's ongoing struggle with environmental damage and failing human health is a major reason the Chinese government has begun to pursue wind power aggressively as an alternative source of the country's energy.

Could Wind Power Save a Mountain?

One of the worst problems with the world's heavy reliance on coal is that certain mining practices irreparably scar the landscape. As buried coal has become harder to reach over the years, traditional underground mining methods have been cast aside for a faster, cheaper method known as mountaintop removal (MTR). According to the National Mining Association, an estimated 15 percent of America's coal production comes from MTR mining, especially in the coal-rich Appalachians. MTR involves stripping trees from forests, drilling holes in rock, and then blasting the mountain apart with dynamite. Following the blast, machines with massive buckets mounted on the front roll in to scoop the coal from the exposed seams. Bob Sloan, an author from Kentucky who has written extensively about how MTR ravages the land, describes the aftermath:

> After the coal is loaded out, the process is repeated until there's no more coal. If there's any mountain left at all, it resembles an Arizona mesa, if one could be found that was the pasty gray of death. Granted, mesas can be lovely things. I have a few times sat someplace in Arizona and watched one of them for hours, transfixed by the eerie loveliness of shifting light and ever changing color on those high rock towers. But what's left behind in the course of mountaintop removal has none of those qualities. Whatever time of day you look at it, the wreckage of a mountain is dead white shale and gravel and rock with no more beauty than a cinderblock.[24]

People throughout Appalachia have fought unsuccessfully for years to save their mountains. Now, an environmental group in West Virginia is fighting to protect Coal River Mountain. The group, Coal River Mountain Watch, proposes that coal mining revert back to the underground method and a wind farm composed of 220 turbines be installed on the mountaintop. A study commissioned by the group showed that a wind farm could produce enough power for 150,000 homes, which is more energy than the surrounding communities currently use. Mary Anne Hilt, executive director of another environmental group, called Appalachian

> **"[Mountaintop removal] involves stripping trees from forests, drilling holes in rock, and then blasting the mountain apart with dynamite."**

Voices, shares her thoughts about the proposal: "If you can build a wind farm in the middle of the Appalachian coalfields on a mountain slated for mountaintop removal, it would be a powerful statement toward making people part of the alternative energy economy."[25]

Curtailing Global Warming

Many scientists and energy experts use global warming as a major example of why wind power is such an important energy source for the future. Because energy generated from wind does not involve burning, no heat-trapping gases such as CO_2 (or any other pollutants) are emitted into the atmosphere. For that reason, the increased use of wind power could drastically reduce the amount of greenhouse gases that are believed to contribute to global warming. The DOE explains: "Supplying 20% of U.S. electricity from wind could reduce annual electric sector carbon dioxide (CO_2) emissions by 825 million metric tons by 2030."[26]

Global warming is a controversial subject because the Earth's climate has fluctuated throughout all of its history, from the Pleistocene epoch (more commonly known as the Ice Age) to later periods when temperatures were much warmer. Scientists are aware of this natural fluctuation, but many say that since the advent of the Industrial Revolution in the mid-eighteenth century, when the use of fossil fuels began to soar, the planet has been warming faster than at any other time in history. The scientists who are most concerned about global warming say this is no coincidence—they are convinced that the Earth is warming rapidly because of the billions of tons of CO_2 that are being pumped into the atmosphere whenever fossil fuels are burned.

> **According to the DOE, electricity generation currently accounts for nearly 50 percent of all water usage in the United States.**

The connection between human activities and atmospheric CO_2 was first suggested in the 1950s by the late scientist Charles David Keeling, who suspected that worldwide industrialization, which involved burning enormous amounts of fossil fuels, had caused abnormally high levels of CO_2 to build up in the atmosphere. After performing years of measurements in a laboratory atop Mauna Loa on the island of Hawaii, Keeling concluded that there was a direct correlation between CO_2 in the atmosphere and fossil fuel burning, and he determined that CO_2 levels were steadily rising. In the years since his findings, researchers on Mauna Loa have continued to measure CO_2 levels and have noted that the levels continue to rise year after year. Many scientists warn that if this continues, global warming will have catastrophic results for the planet—and by turning to wind power and other forms of renewable energy, the damage could be curtailed.

Conserving Water Resources

One important environmental advantage of wind power is that it saves water, which is used prolifically for cooling in natural gas, coal, and nuclear power plants. Windustry states that to produce the same amount of electricity it would take about 500 times more water with coal than wind, and about 600 times more water with nuclear power than wind. According to the DOE, electricity generation currently accounts for nearly 50 percent of all water usage in the United States. The agency states that if wind power were to provide 20 percent of America's energy by 2030, 4 trillion gallons (15 trillion L) of water would be saved.

Wind Power's Effect on Wildlife

People who are not supportive of wind power often point out that wind turbines are hazardous to wild bird populations. This concern is a valid one, but it usually relates to older wind farms such as Altamont Pass Wind Resource Area in California, which opened in 1982 and is one of the oldest in the United States. Due to poor planning, the wind farm's 5,400 turbines were placed directly in a major migratory pathway for birds, and an article in *Popular Mechanics* describes the result: "As it turned out, Altamont Pass could add to its list of pioneering superlatives this frightening title: deadliest wind farm in North America. More than 4700 birds are killed here each year, including 1300 raptors [birds of prey]."[27] According to a report by the California Energy Commission, every year wind turbines at Altamont Pass kill hundreds of golden eagles, red-tailed hawks, burrowing and other owl species, falcons, and vultures. Ecologists are studying the wind turbines to determine which are proving to be deadliest for the birds, and manufacturers are required to take those turbines down or relocate them. This information is also used to plan wind farms that pose a lesser risk to wildlife. Newer turbines, such as those at Buena Vista Wind Farm in Byron, California, are much taller, so they are above the flying range of most birds.

Studies have shown that wind turbines post an even greater risk to bats than to birds. Bats play an extremely important role in nature because they feast on insects that destroy agricultural crops and mosquitoes that can spread disease. Researchers studying unusually high bat mortality at wind farms have long been puzzled by the deaths because bats use radar to avoid flying into stationary objects. Erin Baerwald, a researcher from the University of Calgary in Alberta, Canada, explains: "When people were first starting to talk about the issue, it was 'bats running into the turbine blades.'

> **Studies have shown that wind turbines post an even greater risk to bats than to birds.**

We always said, 'No, bats don't run into things.' Bats can detect and avoid all kinds of structures." A particularly puzzling factor is that many bats found dead beneath wind turbines show no signs of injuries. In August 2008 Baerwald announced that she and fellow researchers believed they had found the cause. They examined the carcasses of hoary and silver-haired bats and discovered that the creatures' lungs had exploded—a condition known as barotrauma—most likely caused by the rapid drop in pressure that occurs as air flows over wind turbine blades. "This kind of answers the mystery," Baerwald says. "It was something nobody could have predicted."[28] Armed with this new information, scientists are starting to look closely at wind farms to determine how the problem can be solved, perhaps by powering turbines down at night and during the fall migration season when bats are most active.

Overcoming the Hurdles

Like all energy sources, wind power is not without its challenges. The world is heavily reliant on fossil fuels, especially coal, and that will not likely change in the near future. But as these fuels grow scarcer, and their burning continues to cause acid rain and other forms of pollution, scientists worldwide tout wind power as a leading choice for environmental protection.

How Does Wind Power Affect the Environment?

"The modern wind turbine is far less harmful to birds than are radio towers, tall buildings, airplanes and vehicles and numerous other manmade objects. Bird deaths due to wind development will never be more than a very small fraction of those caused by other commonly accepted human activities."

—American Wind Energy Association, "Wind Energy and Wildlife: Frequently Asked Questions," June 29, 2005. www.awea.org.

The American Wind Energy Association promotes wind energy as a clean source of electricity for consumers around the world.

"At the current estimated mortality rate, the wind industry will be killing 900,000 to 1.8 million birds per year."

—Donald Michael Fry, "The House Subcommittee on Fisheries, Wildlife and Oceans Oversight Hearing on: 'Gone with the Wind: Impacts of Wind Turbines on Birds and Bats' testimony," May 1, 2007. http://amherstislandwindinfo.com.

Fry is director of the Pesticides and Birds program at the American Bird Conservancy.

Bracketed quotes indicate conflicting positions.

* Editor's Note: While the definition of a primary source can be narrowly or broadly defined, for the purposes of Compact Research, a primary source consists of: 1) results of original research presented by an organization or researcher; 2) eyewitness accounts of events, personal experience, or work experience; 3) first-person editorials offering pundits' opinions; 4) government officials presenting political plans and/or policies; 5) representatives of organizations presenting testimony or policy.

66 In what has to be one of the biggest ironies surrounding alternative energy, many of the objections to wind energy focus on its effect on nature.99

—Joseph Ogando, "Who Will Make All the Wind Turbines?" *Design News*, November 3, 2008.

Ogando is senior editor of *Design News*.

66 Wind-power plants do not produce greenhouse gases, CO_2, [oxides of nitrogen and sulfur], particulate pollutants, or waste products.99

—Stan Gibilisco, *Alternative Energy Demystified*. New York: McGraw-Hill, 2007.

Gibilisco is an electronics engineer, researcher, and mathematician.

66 A study by the National Academy of Sciences found no evidence that wind farms are decreasing bird populations; global warming is a much bigger threat to birds and bats than wind blades.99

—*Los Angeles Times* editorial, "The Renewable Energy Future," September 17, 2007. www.latimes.com.

The *Los Angeles Times* is the second-largest metropolitan newspaper in the United States.

66 Windmills are no panacea either. They are giant bird-killing Cuisinarts, and we'd have to build lots of them to produce significant energy.99

—John Stossel, "The Global Warming Myth?" ABC News, April 20, 2007. http://abcnews.go.com.

Stossel is a news correspondent and coanchor of the television news program *20/20*.

❝In addition to reducing CO_2 wind energy also avoids the emission of toxic chemicals such as mercury and air pollutants such as smog creating nitrogen oxides, acid rain forming sulphur dioxide and particulate deposits.❞

—European Wind Energy Association, "A Cleaner Climate," *Wind Directions*, February/March 2008. www.ewea.org.

The European Wind Energy Association refers to itself as the "voice of the wind industry" for actively promoting the utilization of wind power in Europe and throughout the world.

❝Wind power would be a critical part of a broad and near-term strategy to substantially reduce air pollution, water pollution, and global climate change associated with traditional generation technologies.❞

—U.S. Department of Energy, *20% Wind Energy by 2030*, July 2008. www1.eere.energy.gov.

The Department of Energy's mission is to advance the national, economic, and energy security of the United States.

❝I would simply point out that climate alarmism has become a cottage industry in this country and many others, but a growing number of scientists and the general public are coming around to the idea that climate change is natural and that there is no reason for alarm.❞

—James Inhofe, "Global Warming Alarmism Reaches a 'Tipping Point,'" speech to U.S. Senate, October 26, 2007. http://epw.senate.gov.

Inhofe is a U.S. senator from Oklahoma and a member of the Environment and Public Works Committee.

How Does Wind Power Affect the Environment?

- Wind farms produce **no air or water pollution** because no fuel is burned.

- Coal is known to be the **dirtiest** of all fossil fuels and has been connected with **acid rain**, as well as **air pollution** caused by particulates (soot).

- Worldwatch Institute states that one coal-fired power plant can release as much as **30,000 tons** (27,200 t) of sulfur dioxide into the air each year.

- A controversial study by two researchers at the University of Maryland showed that huge wind turbine installations could **potentially influence weather patterns** by clearing cloudy skies and altering the course of storms.

- The U.S. Department of Energy states that generating **20 percent** of America's electricity from wind power could reduce carbon dioxide emissions by more than **900 million tons** (825 million t) by 2030.

- Coal, nuclear, and gas power plants require massive amounts of water for cooling; according to the U.S. Department of Energy, electricity generation accounts for nearly **50 percent** of all water withdrawals in the United States, and generating **20 percent** of the country's power with wind would save **4 trillion gallons** (15 trillion L) of water by 2030.

Carbon Dioxide Emissions by Sector

Many scientists are concerned that Earth is warming more rapidly than at any period in history, a phenomenon known as global warming. They say that this is largely due to the worldwide burning of fossil fuels, which emits heat-trapping (greenhouse) gases such as carbon dioxide into the atmosphere. That is one of the major reasons why wind power is such a promising source of energy: It requires no burning, so it does not pollute the air or water. This graph shows carbon dioxide emissions in the United States during 2007 by sector.

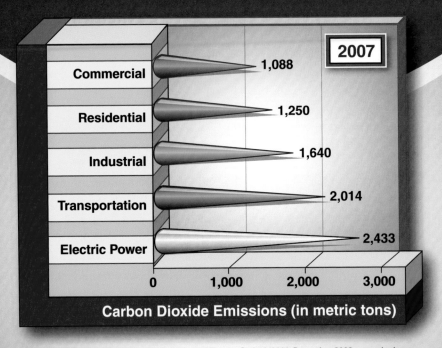

Source: Energy Information Administration, *Annual Energy Outlook 2009*, December 2008. www.eia.doe.gov.

- A March 2007 article in *Christian Science Monitor* stated that at least **37 countries** plan to add coal-fired power plants by the end of 2012, which would pump an additional **9 billion tons** (8.2 billion t) of carbon dioxide into the atmosphere each year.

Wind Power Saves Water

Nuclear power plants and those that generate electricity by burning fossil fuels require a tremendous amount of water for cooling. According to the U.S. Department of Energy, by relying more on wind power and less on fossil fuel power generation, several trillion gallons of water would be saved by 2030. This graph shows the cumulative savings if wind power provides 20 percent of America's power.

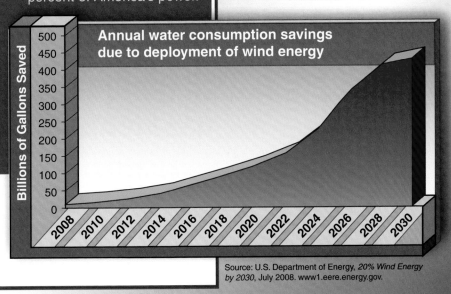

Source: U.S. Department of Energy, *20% Wind Energy by 2030*, July 2008. www1.eere.energy.gov.

- Bird mortality studies have shown that for every 10,000 birds killed by human activities, **fewer than 1 of those deaths is caused by a wind turbine**.

- Coal-fired power plants are one of the leading contributors of **carbon dioxide buildup** in the atmosphere, which is believed to be a strong contributor to global warming.

Wind Turbines and Bird Mortality

One of the main reasons many people object to wind farms is that birds are killed when they collide with turbine blades. This does occur, but it happens much less often than is typically thought. According to the U.S. Department of Energy, for every 10,000 birds killed by all human activity, fewer than 1 is killed by wind turbines. This graph shows the most common causes of bird deaths.

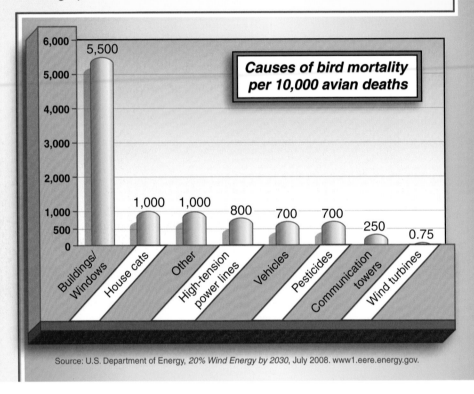

Causes of bird mortality per 10,000 avian deaths

Source: U.S. Department of Energy, *20% Wind Energy by 2030*, July 2008. www1.eere.energy.gov.

- Although nuclear energy is cheaper to produce than wind-generated electricity, nuclear power plants generate **toxic radioactive waste** that is hazardous to the environment.

- A study announced in January 2009 by the British Wind Energy Association found that offshore wind farms in the United Kingdom **pose no risk to marine wildlife and sea birds.**

What Is the Future of Wind Power?

> 66 The potential for wind energy to supply a significant quantity of energy in the United States is enormous. 99
>
> —Charles F. Kutscher, engineer and manager of the Thermal Systems Group at the National Renewable Energy Laboratory in Golden, Colorado.

> 66 Supplying a tiny population over a small amount of land with 25% of its electricity from wind is one thing—doing so over the entire expanse of the United States is quite another. 99
>
> —Jerry Taylor, senior fellow with the Cato Institute.

When a man's entire career has revolved around the oil and gas industries, and in the process he has become a billionaire several times over, he may seem an unlikely candidate to be one of wind power's staunchest supporters. Yet for T. Boone Pickens, there is no question that wind power is the energy of the future—and he is investing tens of millions of dollars to show just how serious he is about it. In July 2008 Pickens announced the "Pickens Plan," which would involve installing thousands of wind turbines (financed by private investors) in the Great Plains area of the United States. Pickens is convinced that wind-generated electricity could replace the electrical power that is currently produced from natural gas and that wind power could supply 20 percent of the United States' energy needs by 2020. He envisions that natural gas would then be used for transportation in order to reduce the demand for gasoline, which is a major by-product of crude oil. The objective, according to the Pickens Plan Web site, "is to underscore the need to declare a national emergency and develop governmental leadership that will address America's staggering dependence on imported oil."[29]

Although Pickens has been criticized by some people for what they see as an unrealistic, even impossible task, especially in such a short time frame, many others have expressed their support. In defense of his plan, Pickens says that wind power is imperative for America's future. He explains: "America is in a hole and it's getting deeper every day. We import 70 percent of our oil at a cost of several hundred billion a year. I've been an oil man all my life, but this is one emergency we can't drill our way out of. But if we create a new renewable energy network, we can break our addiction to foreign oil."[30]

> Pickens is convinced that wind-generated electricity could replace the electrical power that is currently produced from natural gas and that wind power could supply 20 percent of the United States' energy needs by 2020.

In addition to financing a $58 million advertising and Internet education campaign to promote his plan, Pickens is also investing hundreds of millions of dollars to help build a massive wind farm in the Texas Panhandle, an area where there are strong, steady winds. Known as the Pampa Wind Project, the wind farm is being constructed in four phases and is expected to cost about $10 billion. Upon completion in 2014, Pampa will consist of more than 2,500 wind turbines and will generate 4,000 megawatts of electricity—enough to power 1.3 million homes.

A Super-Turbine

Those who object to large wind farms often point out that they require massive amounts of land, along with hundreds of turbines that depend on relatively strong winds in order to operate. The answer could potentially be the MagLev wind turbine, which was created by Chinese developers and perfected by Ed Mazur, the founder of MagLev Wind Turbine Technologies in Sierra Vista, Arizona. An article in *Green Tech Gazette* describes the uniqueness of the turbine: "The MagLev wind turbine is not some flappy-armed giant or tight spinning bird Cuisinart that some environmentalists have objected to having near their back yards or in bird flight paths. Rather the MagLev wind turbine is a compact, self-contained device that uses magnets to lower the resistance needed to turn the flanges and create electricity."[31] The turbine's name comes from how it operates: through magnetic levitation, in which vertically oriented blades are suspended on a cushion of air above the base of the machine.

MagLev's creators claim that the turbine can generate a whopping 1 gigawatt of power—enough to provide electricity to 750,000 homes. That is more power than is produced by 1,000 traditional wind turbines, which, they say, would require about 64,000 acres (26,000 ha) of land compared to fewer than 100 acres (40 ha) for the MagLev. Company officials also say that the MagLev can operate when winds are blowing as

> **MagLev's creators claim that the turbine can generate a whopping 1 gigawatt of power—enough to provide electricity to 750,000 homes.**

slowly as 3.3 miles per hour (1.5 m per second) and as fast as 90 miles per hour (40 m per second). This is different from traditional turbines, most of which require minimum wind speeds of about 10 miles per hour (5.2 m per second) and automatically shut down when winds reach 50 miles per hour (22 m per second). As of January 2009, the MagLev turbine was still in the construction phase, and none had been installed. Although some people are skeptical that the machine will be the super-turbine it is claimed to be, others are convinced that it is the wind turbine of the future.

Ocean Wind Farms

Offshore wind farms are often hailed for their ability to capture ocean winds. The disadvantage, though, is that towers driven into the ocean floor are cost prohibitive to build if they are in water deeper than 65 feet (20 m). Building them in shallower water means that the turbines are likely to be visible from the shoreline, and many people object to that. Also, winds blow up to five times faster over the deep ocean than in shallower water, so the potential is much greater for generating electricity. Another consideration is that the closer the turbines are to shore, the more likely they are to interfere with shipping operations, aircraft and weather radar, and seabird populations. These challenges could potentially be overcome by wind turbines that float on platforms in the deep ocean, rather than being installed on fixed foundations. Researchers at the Massachusetts Institute of Technology (MIT) teamed up with the U.S. National Renewable Energy Laboratory to develop the floating turbines, which many people are calling the next generation of wind power. For years MIT engineer Paul Sclavounos has specialized in designing large floating platforms for deep-sea oil and gas exploration, and he wondered whether the same concept could work with ocean-based wind farms. When this occurred to him, he thought: "Wait a minute. Why can't we simply take those windmills and put them on floaters and move them farther offshore, where there's plenty of space and lots of wind?"[32]

> **Researchers estimate that the floating turbines could be located 100 miles (161 km) from shore, where water is as deep as 650 feet (200 m).**

Sclavounos was convinced that the same concept could indeed work for wind turbines, and he put his talent and expertise into developing the project. The result is a floating turbine that revolves around a tension-leg system, in which a platform floats below the surface of the water and is held rigidly in place by long steel cables (known as tethers) that connect it to steel or concrete anchors driven into the ocean floor. The deeper the water, the longer the tethers need to be. Researchers estimate that the floating turbines could be located 100 miles (161 km) from shore, where water is as deep as 650 feet (200 m). They designed the turbines to be assembled at onshore shipyards because ocean assembly would be extremely expensive due to the turbines' enormous size—nearly 300 feet (90 m) high with blades 450 feet (140 m) across. Once the turbines are assembled, tugboats can tow them out into the ocean to be installed on the platforms.

In December 2007 the Netherlands-based developer Blue H Technologies launched a prototype floating wind turbine 12 miles (19 km) off the coast of southern Italy. The company planned to have the full-size turbine in place in 2009 and eventually hopes to expand it into a full wind farm. Blue H also plans to install 120 floating turbines in deep water 23 miles (37 km) off the coast of Martha's Vineyard in Massachusetts and is exploring other locations as well.

Futuristic Sailing

Using the wind to propel boats across the water is certainly not a new concept. People have sailed with the wind for thousands of years, and sailing is still an extremely popular form of boating. But for the world's estimated 50,000 merchant ships, which travel the ocean carrying everything from crude oil, grain, and timber to motor vehicles and electronic equipment, relying on the wind has long been considered antiquated—although that may change in the near future.

A German company known as SkySails has developed gigantic kite sails that can be launched high in the air from the bow of all kinds of oceangoing ships, from small fishing trawlers to megafreighters, with the size of the sails varying based on the size of the ship. Once the kite is in the air, it flies from 300 to 1,600 feet (100 to 500 m) above sea level, where the winds are about 50 percent stronger than they are closer to the water's surface. The sails are controlled by a computer that operates much like an airplane's autopilot system, constantly monitoring and recording measurements to keep the kite in the optimal position to best propel the ship.

> " A German company known as SkySails has developed gigantic kite sails that can be launched high in the air from the bow of all kinds of oceangoing ships, from small fishing trawlers to megafreighters. "

There are several advantages to the SkySails concept, one of which is fuel savings. Fuel costs for commercial shipping have more than doubled in the past few years, and SkySails claims that its kite sail can cut fuel consumption by as much as 35 percent. There are also environmental benefits. Each year oceangoing ships pump an estimated 800 million

> **The innovative wind turbine has rotors that are bent into a ball shape so they move parallel to the wind, and it capitalizes on a kind of physics known as the Venturi effect.**

tons (726 million t) of carbon dioxide into the atmosphere, which represents about 5 percent of the world's total emissions. By burning less fuel, the ships' emissions could be drastically reduced, which could help reduce global warming.

During January and February 2008, the world's first kite-powered commercial ship, the MV *Beluga SkySails*, made its maiden voyage from Germany to Venezuela. By the time it was back in port, officials estimated that the fuel savings totaled from $1,000 and $1,500 per day. In October 2008 the U.S. Navy announced that it had chartered the MV *Beluga SkySails* to carry military equipment from several European ports to the United States, and it hopes to realize significant fuel savings as well.

Homegrown Wind Power

Much of the publicity about wind power revolves around huge wind farms and the important role they play in generating the world's electricity. But the future also looks bright for individual homeowners because of technological developments on a smaller scale. One example is the Energy Ball, which was developed by the Netherlands-based Home Energy International. The innovative wind turbine has rotors that are bent into a ball shape so they move parallel to the wind and capitalize on a kind of physics known as the Venturi effect. In a *Live Science* article, journalist Michael Schirber explains: "The Venturi effect is characterized by a low pressure that occurs when a flow of air or liquid speeds up as it is constricted. Some perfume bottles use the Venturi effect to suck up perfume into the spray nozzle. The Energy Ball's design constricts the wind, thereby causing the pressure to drop inside the ball. This sucks in air flowing around the ball and helps turn the rotor blades."[33]

According to researchers at Technical University of Delft in the Netherlands, the Energy Ball's sucking action causes it to use more of the wind and therefore makes it about 40 percent more efficient than a propeller-style turbine of the same size. The machines can be installed on a pole or on top of a flat roof, and in places where the wind is relatively strong, they can supply up to 1,750 kilowatt-hours of electricity per year, or about 15 percent of what the average household uses.

Another wind power innovation is the WindTronics 760, also known as a "wind turbine in a box." Manufactured by a Michigan company called EarthTronics, the round-shaped turbine is just 5 feet (1.5 m) in diameter and can generate nearly 1,600 kilowatt-hours of electricity per year. It can operate when wind speeds are as slow as 3 miles per hour (1.3 m per second) and has no upper limit, so faster winds will not cause it to shut down.

How Windy Will the Future Be?

There are numerous reasons why the world is growing more reliant on wind power. The wind is a clean source of energy that emits no pollutants into the atmosphere, it is renewable, and it has the proven ability to supplement—or, as some believe, even replace—fossil fuels to generate electricity. Those who are most enthusiastic about wind power say that only a fraction of its potential has been tapped and that with ample financial investment and commitment, it can become one of the world's leading energy sources.

Many challenges remain, but challenges are nothing new where advances in technology are concerned. Hurdles can be overcome, as they have in the past. As author Robert L. Evans writes: "Fortunately, man is by nature a problem-solving species, and there are many possible solutions in which future energy supplies can be made sustainable for future generations."[34]

What Is the Future of Wind Power?

"Areas with good wind resources have the potential to supply up to 20% of the electricity consumption of the United States."

—White House National Economic Council, *Advanced Energy Initiative*, February 2006. www.whitehouse.gov.

The National Economic Council advises the president of the United States on matters related to U.S. and global economic policy.

"Wind power cannot produce dependably or independently, and consistently fails to live up to even its own low expectations."

—Sue Sliwinski, "Wind Power Is Not the Answer Advocates Claim It Is," *Buffalo (NY) News*, January 2, 2009. www.buffalonews.com.

Sliwinski is a board member with National Wind Watch.

"Embracing wind energy today will lay the foundation for a healthy tomorrow."

—Windustry, "Learn About Wind Energy," 2008. www.windustry.org.

Through research, education, and advocacy efforts, Windustry seeks to promote progressive renewable energy solutions.

Bracketed quotes indicate conflicting positions.

* Editor's Note: While the definition of a primary source can be narrowly or broadly defined, for the purposes of Compact Research, a primary source consists of: 1) results of original research presented by an organization or researcher; 2) eyewitness accounts of events, personal experience, or work experience; 3) first-person editorials offering pundits' opinions; 4) government officials presenting political plans and/or policies; 5) representatives of organizations presenting testimony or policy.

66 The energy challenges our country faces are severe and have gone unaddressed for far too long. Our addiction to foreign oil doesn't just undermine our national security and wreak havoc on our environment—it cripples our economy and strains the budgets of working families all across America. 99

—TheWhite House, "The Agenda: Energy and the Environment," January 2009. www.whitehouse.gov.

The White House Web site presents the Obama administration's positions on energy and many other issues.

66 Through continued [research and development] and infrastructure development, great strides will be made to produce even more advanced machines supporting future deployment of wind power technology. 99

—U.S. Department of Energy, *20% Wind Energy by 2030*, July 2008. www1.eere.energy.gov.

The Department of Energy's mission is to advance the national, economic, and energy security of the United States.

66 In the long term, wind will be the most important single source of electricity generation. 99

—Sven Teske, *Energy Revolution*, October 2008. www.greenpeace.org.

Teske is the international renewable energy director with Greenpeace.

66 Wind generates only when it is blowing, and it blows least when power is most valuable. 99

—Robert J. Michaels, "Renewables Aren't the Answer," *USA Today*, October 20, 2008. http://blogs.usatoday.com.

Michaels is an economics professor at California State University–Fullerton and an adjunct scholar at the Cato Institute.

66 We can continue down this destructive, business-as-usual path of building coal plants, at the expense of our environment.... Or we can adopt policies that will encourage renewable energy investments, thereby reducing the cost of energy, creating thousands of sustainable jobs, and vastly improving the quality of our environment and public health. 99

—Kerwin Olson, "Let's Invest in Wind, Instead of Coal," *Indianapolis Business Journal*, November 3, 2008.

Olson is program director of the Citizens Action Coalition.

66 I think it would be a thing of beauty if, when Lady Liberty looks out on the horizon, she not only welcomes new immigrants, but lights their way with a torch powered by an ocean windfarm. 99

—Michael Bloomberg, "Mayor Bloomberg Announces New York City's First Steps Toward Developing Off-Shore Windfarms and Other Sources of Renewable Energy at 2008 National Clean Energy Summit," August 19, 2008. www.nyc.gov.

Bloomberg is the mayor of New York City.

66 The carbon-free power technologies that the nation should focus on deploying right now at large scale are efficiency, wind power, and solar power.... They could easily provide the vast majority of new [power] generation for the next quarter century and beyond. 99

—Joseph Romm, "Statement Before the Committee on Environment and Public Works, Subcommittee on Clean Air and Nuclear Safety of the United States Senate," July 16, 2008. www.americanprogressaction.org.

Romm is senior fellow at the Center for American Progress Action Fund.

What Is the Future of Wind Power?

- A 2006 study by the U.S. Department of Energy, General Electric, and the Massachusetts Institute of Technology showed that offshore wind resources on the Atlantic and Pacific coasts **exceed the current electricity produced** by the entire U.S. power industry.

- The American Wind Energy Association states that if the wind industry were to consistently grow at **18 percent per year, 6 percent** of the electricity in the United States could be generated by wind power by 2020.

- The U.S. Department of Energy projects that **20 percent** of America's electricity will be generated by wind power by the year 2030.

- Denmark's goal is to increase its energy production from wind power to **50 percent** by 2025, mostly from offshore installations.

- At the end of 2007, China's installed wind power totaled over **6 gigawatts**, making the country the fifth-largest producer after Germany, the United States, Spain, and India.

- A November 2008 report by the North American Electric Reliability Corporation stated that increased electricity generation from solar and wind power could **increase the frequency of blackouts** and **reduce the reliability** of America's electricity grid.

Cutting CO₂ Emissions with Wind Power

The U.S. Department of Energy has set an aggressive goal for wind power in the United States to generate 20 percent of the country's electricity by 2030. If that goal is achieved, it would keep an estimated 8.4 billion tons of carbon dioxide out of the atmosphere. This graph shows the cumulative CO_2 emissions that would be avoided from 2008 to 2030.

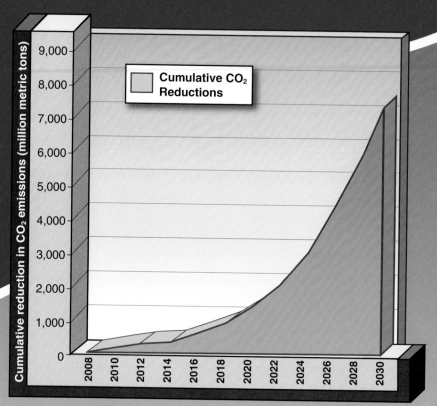

Source: U.S. Department of Energy, *20% Wind Energy by 2030*, July 2008. www1.eere.energy.gov.

- According to the American Wind Energy Association, if wind energy generated 560 billion kilowatt-hours of electricity (15 percent of the U.S. total), only **0.6 percent** of the land in the lower 48 states would have to be developed to accommodate wind farms.

America Is an Emerging Wind Power Leader

Even though for years the United States has lagged behind other countries in terms of its exploitation of wind power, in 2007 the country led the world in new wind power installations, with 5,244 megawatts,* which represented 26 percent of new global wind power. This chart shows the top 10 countries and how they ranked for new installations The number after each country represents that country's new installations during 2007.

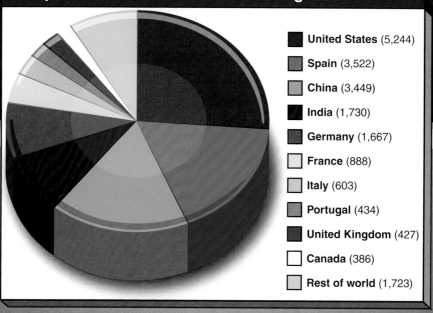

Top-10 new wind installations during 2007

- United States (5,244)
- Spain (3,522)
- China (3,449)
- India (1,730)
- Germany (1,667)
- France (888)
- Italy (603)
- Portugal (434)
- United Kingdom (427)
- Canada (386)
- Rest of world (1,723)

*Note: Electricity generating capacity is measured in watts and is an expression of instantaneous power output. A kilowatt is 1,000 watts, a megawatt is 1 million watts, and a gigawatt is 1 billion watts. A kilowatt hour is an expression of energy produced over time. For example a 1,000 watt generator that operates for an entire day would produce 24,000 watt-hours (24 kilowatt hours) of energy.

Source: Global Wind Energy Council, "US, China & Spain Lead World Wind Power Market in 2007," February 6, 2008. www.ewea.org.

- Wind power in the United States is expected to grow by **7,800 megawatts** in 2009, which is the equivalent of the energy produced by 9 nuclear reactors.

Global Support for Renewable Energy

A 2008 poll conducted by WorldOpinion.org, a collaborative project that involves research centers from around the world, involved nearly 21,000 participants from 21 countries.

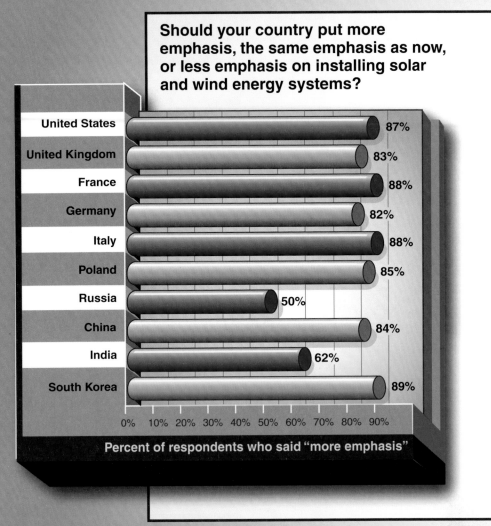

Should your country put more emphasis, the same emphasis as now, or less emphasis on installing solar and wind energy systems?

Country	Percent
United States	87%
United Kingdom	83%
France	88%
Germany	82%
Italy	88%
Poland	85%
Russia	50%
China	84%
India	62%
South Korea	89%

Percent of respondents who said "more emphasis"

Source: WorldPublicOpinion.org, "World Publics Strongly Favor Requiring More Wind and Solar Energy, More Efficiency, Even If It Increases Costs," November 19, 2008.

Building nuclear power plants?

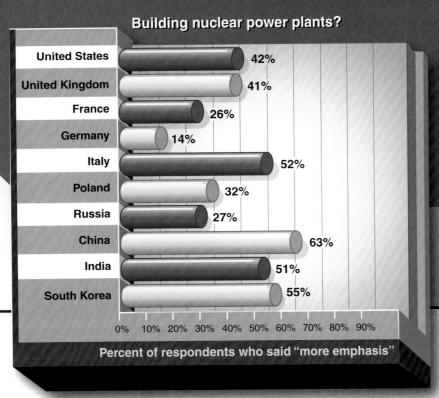

Country	Percent
United States	42%
United Kingdom	41%
France	26%
Germany	14%
Italy	52%
Poland	32%
Russia	27%
China	63%
India	51%
South Korea	55%

Percent of respondents who said "more emphasis"

Building coal- and oil-fired power plants?

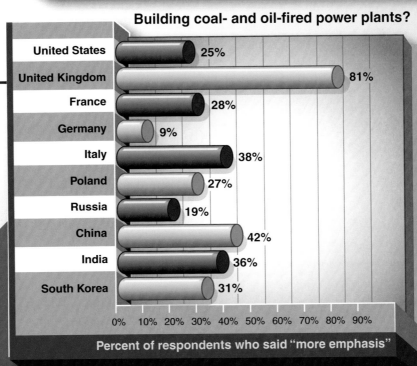

Country	Percent
United States	25%
United Kingdom	81%
France	28%
Germany	9%
Italy	38%
Poland	27%
Russia	19%
China	42%
India	36%
South Korea	31%

Percent of respondents who said "more emphasis"

Key People and Advocacy Groups

American Wind Energy Association: The AWEA, which refers to itself as the "hub of the wind energy industry," promotes wind energy as a clean source of electricity for consumers around the world.

Erin Baerwald: A researcher from the University of Calgary in Alberta, Canada, Baerwald was instrumental in the discovery that bats killed on wind farms died when air pressure caused their lungs to explode, rather than from colliding with turbines.

Charles F. Brush: An inventor from Cleveland, Ohio, Brush built the first large windmill that was capable of generating electricity in 1888.

John Burnham: An American engineer, during the mid-1800s Burnham came up with a concept for a windmill that would change wind directions and control wind speed without human attention.

Georges Darrieus: A French engineer, Darrieus designed and patented a vertical-axis wind turbine in 1931 that became known as the Darrieus model.

Daniel Halladay: A mechanic from New England, Halladay designed the windmill that was envisioned by his associate, John Burnham.

National Renewable Energy Laboratory: An agency of the U.S. Department of Energy, the NREL is the United States' primary laboratory for renewable energy and energy efficiency research and development.

T. Boone Pickens: An American billionaire who made his fortune in the oil and gas industries, Pickens is a staunch supporter of wind power.

Eric Rosenbloom: The founder of National Wind Watch, Rosenbloom is a science editor from Vermont who opposes the expansion of wind power.

Windustry: Through research, education, and advocacy efforts, Windustry seeks to promote progressive renewable energy solutions.

Chronology

1888
Charles F. Brush, an inventor from Cleveland, Ohio, develops the first large windmill that can generate electricity.

1854
Daniel Halladay, a mechanic from Connecticut, develops an innovative windmill that can automatically turn to face changing wind directions and control the speed of its own wheel so it does not spin too fast in high winds.

1893
The World's Columbian Exhibition is held in Chicago, Illinois, where 15 windmill companies showcase their goods.

500–900
The first windmills are developed in Persia (now Iran) and used for grinding grain and pumping water.

500

1800

1900

1600s
European settlers in America use wind power to grind grain and pump water, as well as to cut wood at sawmills.

1931
The first vertical-axis windmill is patented by French engineer Georges Darrieus.

1859
Edward L. Drake is the first to drill for oil on his land near Titusville, Pennsylvania (which is a radical concept for the time); he strikes oil and successfully pumps it to the surface.

1941
The Grandpa's Knob wind turbine, located on a hilltop in Rutland, Vermont, supplies electricity to the local community for several months during World War II.

1973
The Organization of Petroleum Exporting Countries
(OPEC) oil embargo causes
oil prices to spike, resulting
in increased interest in wind
power and other renewable
energy sources.

2007
The United States becomes
the world leader in new
wind power installations.

1990
More than 2,200 megawatts
of wind power is installed
in California, represent-
ing more than half of the
world's estimated capacity
at the time.

2004
Worldwide installed
wind-generated
electricity reaches
30,000 megawatts.

1970   1990   2000   2010

2003
The United States' total installed
wind-generated electricity capacity
reaches nearly 5,000 megawatts.

2006
Wind turbines in the United States generate a total
of 26.6 billion kilowatt-hours of electricity, enough
to power more than 2.4 million households.

2008
British Petroleum reports that worldwide oil and coal
consumption is outpacing annual production, with the
demand for coal rising for the fifth consecutive year.

2009
President Barack Obama announces that he
wants to double wind, solar, and geothermal
energy production in the United States by 2012.

Related Organizations

American Council on Renewable Energy (ACORE)

1600 K St. NW, Suite 700

Washington, DC 20006

phone: (202) 393-0001 • fax: (202) 393-0606

e-mail: info@acore.org • Web site: www.acore.org

ACORE works to bring all forms of renewable energy into the mainstream of America's economy and lifestyle. Its Web site offers news releases, policy descriptions, reports, and links to articles.

American Wind Energy Association (AWEA)

501 M St. NW, Suite 1000

Washington, DC 20005

phone: (202) 383-2500 • fax: (202) 383-2505

e-mail: windmail@awea.org • Web site: www.awea.org

AWEA promotes wind energy as a clean source of electricity for consumers around the world and refers to itself as the "hub of the wind energy industry." Its Web site offers a collection of fact sheets, the *Wind Energy Weekly* newsletter, articles, policy statements, and news releases.

Energy Efficiency and Renewable Energy (EERE)

Mail Stop EE-1

Department of Energy

Washington, DC 20585

phone: (877) 337-3463

Web site: www.eere.energy.gov

An agency of the U.S. Department of Energy, the EERE seeks to enhance energy efficiency and productivity; bring clean, reliable, and affordable energy technologies to the marketplace; and make a positive difference in Americans' lives by enhancing their energy choices and quality of life. Available on its Web site are speeches, congressional testimonies, news articles, news releases, and a search engine that retrieves numerous publications related to wind power.

European Wind Energy Association (EWEA)

Rue d'Arlon 63-65

B-1040 Brussels

Belgium

phone: +32 2 546 1940 • fax: +32 2 546 1944

e-mail: ewea@ewea.org • Web site: www.ewea.org

The EWEA actively promotes the utilization of wind power in Europe and throughout the world. Its Web site offers statistical documents, news releases, articles, videos, a Myths & Benefits section, and policy statements.

Interstate Renewable Energy Council (IREC)

PO Box 1156

Latham, NY 12110-1156

phone: (518) 458-6059

e-mail: info@irecusa.org • Web site: www.irecusa.org

The IREC's mission is to accelerate the sustainable use of renewable energy sources and technologies in and through state and local government and community activities. Its Web site offers three different newsletters, a resources section with various publications, and links to related sites.

National Association of Energy Service Companies (NAESCO)

1615 M St. NW, Suite 900

Washington, DC 20036

phone: (202) 822-0950 • fax: (202) 822-0955

e-mail: info@naesco.org • Web site: www.naesco.org

NAESCO's mission is to promote efficiency as the first priority in a portfolio of economic and environmentally sustainable energy resources, as well as to encourage customers and public officials to consider energy efficiency when they are making energy choices. Its Web site features news articles, news releases, a newsletter, and a resources section that has various publications.

National Energy Education Development (NEED) Project

8408 Kao Circle

Manassas, VA 20110

phone: (703) 257-1117 • fax: (703) 257-0037

e-mail: info@need.org • Web site: www.need.org

The NEED Project seeks to make energy education a priority in schools and colleges throughout the United States. Its Web site features a number of NEED Energy InfoBooks for students of all ages, energy polls, the *Energy Exchange* and *Career Currents* newsletters, a searchable energy bibliography, and news releases.

National Renewable Energy Laboratory (NREL)

1617 Cole Blvd.

Golden, CO 80401-3393

phone: (303) 275-3000

e-mail: info@nrel.gov • Web site: www.nrel.gov

The NREL is the United States' primary laboratory for renewable energy and energy efficiency research and development. Its Web site offers a wide variety of information about wind power and other types of renewable energy, including a Student Resources on Renewable Energy section.

National Wind Watch

PO Box 293

Rowe, MA 01367

Web site: www.wind-watch.org

National Wind Watch is a coalition of groups and individuals who seek to promote awareness of and document the negative aspects of industrial-scale wind turbines on the environment, economy, and quality of life. Its Web site features articles, technical papers, news releases, fact sheets, and a Fast Facts section.

Windustry

2105 First Ave. South

Minneapolis, MN 55404

phone: (612) 870-3461 • toll free: (800) 946-3640

fax: (612) 813-5612

e-mail: info@windustry.org • Web site: www.windustry.org

Through research, education, and advocacy efforts, Windustry seeks to promote progressive renewable energy solutions. Its Web site features policy information, research papers, newsletters, and a *Wind Basics* series designed to help people learn about wind power.

Worldwatch Institute

1776 Massachusetts Ave. NW

Washington, DC 20036-1904

phone: (202) 452-1999 • fax: (202) 296-7365

e-mail: worldwatch@worldwatch.org • Web site: www.worldwatch.org

Worldwatch focuses on challenges such as climate change, resource degradation, population growth, and poverty, by developing and disseminating data and strategies for achieving a sustainable society. Its Web site features the *Eye on Earth* magazine, news releases, annual reports, and a collection of informative publications available for purchase.

For Further Research

Books

Godfrey Boyle, ed., *Renewable Energy*. New York: Oxford University Press, 2004.

Dan Chiras, *Power from the Wind: Achieving Energy Independence*. Gabriola, BC: New Society, 2009.

David Craddock, *Renewable Energy Made Easy: Free Energy from Solar, Wind, Hydropower, and Other Alternative Energy Sources*. Ocala, FL: Atlantic, 2008.

Robert L. Evans, *Fueling Our Future: An Introduction to Sustainable Energy*. Cambridge: Cambridge University Press, 2007.

Rex Ewing, *Power with Nature: Solar and Wind Energy Demystified*. Masonville, CO: PixyJack, 2003.

Stan Gibilisco, *Alternative Energy Demystified*. New York: McGraw Hill, 2007.

S.L. Klein, *Power to Change the World*. Charleston, SC: BookSurge, 2008.

Joseph Szarka, *Wind Power in Europe*. New York: Palgrave Macmillan, 2007.

Periodicals

Kent Garber, "A Mighty Gust from Texas: Why a Famed Oilman Is Wind Power's Best Hope," *U.S. News & World Report*, September 1, 2008.

Beth Geiger, "Wind at Work: Wind Can Power Storms, Make Electricity, and Carve Rock. It Can Also Whip Up Some Wild Fun," *National Geographic Explorer*, September 2008.

Fred Hapgood, "Windmills in the Sky," *Discover*, October 2008.

Charles J. Murray, "Capturing the Wind," *Design News*, November 3, 2008.

Greg Pahl, "Community Supported Wind Power: It's Been Done Successfully for Decades in Denmark and Many Other European Countries, So Why Not North America?" *Mother Earth News*, June/July 2008.

Megan Phelps, "Why Wind Power Works for Schools," *Mother Earth News*, October/November 2008.

Bobette Riner, "Wind May Be Salvation of Aging U.S. Power Grid," *Natural Gas Week*, June 23, 2008.

Derrick Teal, "Creating a Rustle: Why Some People Just Don't Like Wind," *Environmental Design & Construction*, November 2008.

Leland Teschler, "Inside an Advanced Wind Turbine," *Machine Design*, June 5, 2008.

Richard F. Timmons, "Wind Turbines Offer a Breath of Fresh Air," *Railway Age*, October 2008.

Joe Truini, "Wind, Nature Groups Join Forces to Protect Bats," *Waste News*, October 22, 2008.

Todd Woody, "Trying to Catch the Wind," *Fortune*, November 10, 2008.

Internet Sources

Michael Brenner, *Wind Farms and Radar*, January 2008. www.fas.org/irp/agency/dod/jason/wind.pdf.

Global Wind Energy Council, *Global Wind 2007 Report*, May 2008. www.gwec.net/fileadmin/documents/test2/gwec-08-update_FINAL.pdf.

Steve Hamm, "Wind. The Power. The Promise. The Business," *BusinessWeek*, July 3, 2008. www.businessweek.com/magazine/content/08_27/b4091046392398.htm?chan=magazine+channel_in+depth.

Julia Layton, "How Wind Power Works," How Stuff Works, 2007. http://science.howstuffworks.com/wind-power.htm.

Sven Teske, *Energy Revolution*, October 2008. www.greenpeace.org/raw/content/international/press/reports/energyrevolutionreport.pdf.

Brian Unwin, "Sea Eagles Being Killed by Wind Turbines, *Daily Telegraph*, June 27, 2007. www.telegraph.co.uk/earth/wildlife/3298513/Sea-eagles-being-killed-by-wind-turbines.html.

U.S. Department of Energy, *20% Wind Energy by 2030*, July 2008. www1.eere.energy.gov/windandhydro/pdfs/41869.pdf.

Matt Vella, "Humdinger's Wind Power Alternative," *BusinessWeek*, October 7, 2008. www.businessweek.com/innovate/content/oct2008/id2008106_231604.htm?campaign_id=rss_innovate.

Windustry, "Learn About Wind Energy," 2008. www.windustry.org/wind-basics/learn-about-wind-energy/learn-about-wind-energy.

Source Notes

Overview

1. Timothy B. Hurst, "Vertical Axis Wind Turbines: The Future of Micro Wind?" CleanTechnica, June 20, 2008. http://cleantechnica.com.
2. U.S. Department of Energy and Massachusetts Technology Collaborative, *A Framework for Offshore Wind Energy Development in the United States*, September 2005. www.masstech.org.
3. Windustry, "Learn About Wind Energy," 2008. www.windustry.org.
4. Windustry, "Learn About Wind Energy."
5. Brittany Marquis, "Venturi Eclectic, the World's First Production Solar-Electric Car: Test Drive," *Popular Mechanics*, October 3, 2007. www.popularmechanics.com.
6. Windustry, "Learn About Wind Energy."
7. State Energy Conservation Office, "Texas Wind Energy," 2008. www.seco.cpa.state.tx.us.
8. Jeffrey Logan and Stan Mark Kaplan, "Wind Power in the United States," *CRS Report for Congress*, June 20, 2008. www.fas.org.
9. American Wind Energy Association, "Wind Power Myths vs. Facts," 2005. www.awea.org.
10. Logan and Kaplan, "Wind Power in the United States."
11. Nina Pierpont, "Wind Turbine Syndrome," Testimony before the New York State Legislature Energy Committee, March 7, 2006. www.savewesternny.org.
12. Windustry, "Learn About Wind Energy."

Can Wind Power Supply the World's Energy Needs?

13. Quoted in T. Lindsay Baker, *A Field Guide to American Windmills*. Norman: University of Oklahoma Press, 1985, p. 7.
14. Quoted in Stephanie Busari, "U.S., China Lead Way in Tapping Wind Power," CNN, July 28, 2008. www.cnn.com.
15. Junfeng Li, "Opinion: China's Wind Power Development Exceeds Expectations," WorldWatch Institute, June 2, 2008. www.worldwatch.org.
16. Quoted in Frank Morris, "Missouri Town Is Running on Vapor—and Thriving," National Public Radio, December 30, 2008. www.npr.org.

Can Wind Power Reduce Dependence on Fossil Fuels?

17. Martin Hoffert, interview with author, October 11, 2008.
18. U.S. Department of Energy, "How Fossil Fuels Were Formed." http://fossil.energy.gov.
19. Hoffert, interview.
20. Hoffert, interview.
21. Windustry, "Learn About Wind Energy."

How Does Wind Power Affect the Environment?

22. Alliance for Clean Energy New York, "Wind Power Overview," 2008. www.aceny.org.
23. Keith Bradsher and David Barboza, "Pollution from Chinese Coal Casts a Global Shadow," *New York Times*, June 11, 2006. www.nytimes.com.
24. Bob Sloan, interview with author,

January 8, 2009.

25. Quoted in Peter Slavin, "How Wind Farms May Really Replace Coal Mining," AlterNet, August 19, 2008. www.alternet.org.

26. U.S. Department of Energy, *20% Wind Energy by 2030*. www1.eere.energy.gov.

27. Jennifer Bogo, "How the Deadliest Wind Farm Can Save the Birds: Green Machines," *Popular Mechanics*, September 14, 2007. www.popularmechanics.com.

28. Quoted in Jessica Marshall, "Wind Turbines Kill Bats Without Impact," Discovery Channel, August 25, 2008. http://dsc.discovery.com.

What Is the Future of Wind Power?

29. "T. Boone Pickens Unveils *The Pickens Plan*—a Sweeping, Innovative Plan to Address National Energy Dependency Crisis," PickensPlan, 2008. http://media.pickensplan.com.

30. T. Boone Pickens, "T. Boone Pickens Promotes Energy Plan for America," August 2008. www.boonepickens.com.

31. *Green Tech Gazette*, "Magnetic Wind Turbine Blows Away Competition," November 10, 2007. www.greentechgazette.com.

32. Quoted in Nancy Stauffer, "Floating Wind Turbines the Wave of the Future," *Renewable Energy World*, September 21, 2006. www.renewableenergyworld.com.

33. Michael Schirber, "How an Eggbeater Could Power the Future," *Live Science*, September 10, 2008. www.livescience.com.

34. Robert L. Evans, *Fueling Our Future*. New York: Cambridge University Press, 2007, p. 8.

List of Illustrations

Index

About the Author

Peggy J. Parks holds a bachelor of science degree from Aquinas College in Grand Rapids, Michigan, where she graduated magna cum laude. She has written more than 75 nonfiction educational books for children and young adults, and has published a cookbook called *Welcome Home: Recipes, Memories, and Traditions from the Heart*. Parks lives in Muskegon, Michigan, a town that she says inspires her writing because of its location on the shores of Lake Michigan.